# The Access Manual

Second Edition

From the reviews of the First Edition:

'Both authors are well known for their work on access . . . between them they have produced a useful book that is helpful in the context of our current built environment and what steps can be taken to improve access.'
*Barrierfree*

'This is a well written and practical manual, recommended reading for building engineers concerned with the creation, planning and management of buildings.'
*Building Engineer*

'Incredibly informative . . . will enable you to keep the edge over non-enlightened competitors'
*Architectural Technology*

'This is an excellent book'
*Access Journal*

# The Access Manual

Auditing and managing inclusive built environments

Second Edition

**Ann Sawyer**
Architect and Access Consultant

and

**Keith Bright**
Chartered Building Surveyor and Registered Access Consultant

**Blackwell** Publishing

© 2007 by Blackwell Publishing Ltd

Editorial Offices:
Blackwell Publishing Ltd, 9600 Garsington Road, Oxford OX4 2DQ, UK
  Tel: +44 (0)1865 776868
Blackwell Publishing Inc., 350 Main Street, Malden, MA 02148-5020, USA
  Tel: +1 781 388 8250
Blackwell Publishing Asia Pty Ltd, 550 Swanston Street, Carlton, Victoria 3053,
Australia
  Tel: +61 (0)3 8359 1011

First edition published 2004 by Blackwell Publishing Ltd
This edition published 2007

ISBN-10: 1-4051-4626-5
ISBN-13: 978-1-4051-4626-5

Library of Congress Cataloging-in-Publication Data
  Sawyer, Ann.
  The access manual : auditing and managing inclusive built environments /
  Ann Sawyer, Keith Bright. – 2nd ed.
        p.  cm.
  Includes bibliographical references and index.
  ISBN-13: 978-1-4051-4626-5 (pbk. : alk. paper)
  ISBN-10: 1-4051-4626-5 (pbk. : alk. paper)  1. Barrier-free design–Great Britain–
  Handbooks, manuals, etc.  2. Architectural design–Great Britain–Handbooks,
  manuals, etc.  3. Building laws–Great Britain–Handbooks, manuals, etc.
  I. Bright, Keith.  II. Title.
    NA2545.P5S29  2006
    720.87–dc22
  2006017369

A catalogue record for this title is available from the British Library

Set in 12/15pt Optima
by Graphicraft Limited, Hong Kong
Printed and bound in Singapore
by COS Printers Pte Ltd

The publisher's policy is to use permanent paper from mills that operate a sustainable
forestry policy, and which has been manufactured from pulp processed using acid-free
and elementary chlorine-free practices. Furthermore, the publisher ensures that the text
paper and cover board used have met acceptable environmental accreditation
standards.

For further information on Blackwell Publishing, visit our website:
www.blackwellpublishing.com/construction

# Contents

Sample access audit reports and access statements can be found
on website www.blackwellpublishing.com/theaccessmanual

'Good design should be for everyone'

Daniel Libeskind

# About the authors

**Ann Sawyer** BA Dip. Arch. is an architect and independent access consultant. She works with architects, developers, building owners and facilities managers providing access consultancy services on new and existing buildings and environments. She advises on access and inclusive design, provides access appraisals and audits, advises on improvements to meet new legislative requirements and provides training in accessible design, auditing and the management of accessible environments. She has been involved in many prestigious new build and refurbishment projects for public and private sector clients and has advised on access to a wide variety of historic buildings. Ann is a member of the CABE Enabling Panel and the South East Regional Design Panel.

Ann can be contacted on a.sawyer@blueyonder.co.uk and more information about her work and consultancy services offered can be obtained from www.accessdesign.co.uk

**Keith Bright** is Emeritus Professor of Inclusive Environments at the University of Reading and Visiting Professor of Inclusive Environments in the School of Art and Design at the University of Ulster. He is also a Director of KBC Ltd, an independent access consultancy.

He is a member of the Inclusive Environments Group (IEG), set up under the Commission for Architecture and the Built Environment (CABE) to advise government on the provision and management of inclusive built environments, and is a member of CABE Space Strategic Enabling Panel. Keith is also a member of several British Standard committees developing best practice guidance for the provision of inclusive environments.

He has published widely in academic and practice journals and is the author and editor of several highly regarded reference books related to the development of inclusive environments. He is a regular speaker at national and international conferences on topics related to disability discrimination and the provision and management of inclusive, accessible environments.

Keith can be contacted on info.kbc@btinternet.com and more information about his work can be obtained from www.keithbrightconsultants.com

# Foreword

Spaces and places should inspire and excite. Well designed environments should be easy to use and welcoming. At CABE we aim to influence and educate designers and architects, from both the public and the private sector, to design environments that meet the needs of all their users. Designing and managing environments which enable physical, intellectual, cultural and emotional access requires an understanding of the barriers that many of us experience every day.

With CABE's Inclusive Environment Group we have a new forum in which to open up the debate around inclusive design, to challenge assumptions and explore new ways of doing things. We are working with our partners to deliver the message that inclusive design benefits everyone.

We are all part of an ever-ageing population so we all have good reason to support the changing housing, workplace and leisure needs this demographic shift is bringing about. This places an onus on designers, architects and others involved in the design and maintenance of the built environment to think creatively in order to bring about an accessible public realm for everyone.

We strongly believe that design should always be judged by whether or not it results in an inclusive environment. Good design should reflect the diversity of people who use it and not impose any kind of barriers.

We don't think awareness of these principles is high enough yet. Nobody sets out deliberately to design a poor building or public space. Yet they are all designed and many of them are not accessible. Our Design Review Panel sees a lot of plans for new development. Many of them fall short on inclusive design. Those that achieve compliance with legislation and standards often do so in ways which are joyless and penny-pinching.

Places that work for people need to be designed and managed effectively to enable them to use the space with confidence and dignity. Ensuring we create environments which respond to the needs of the community takes time and requires active participation. Involving people within the design process is the first step to developing environments with people at their centre. Inclusive design needs to inspire good design and not be seen as an afterthought.

I welcome this book because it's about learning from people's individual needs about how to improve everyone's quality of life. That is what is needed to make those inspiring, inclusive, exciting places which CABE champions. Please make the most of what you find in this volume, but please don't use it merely to achieve compliance. Use it to spark creativity, humanity and urbanity in the buildings and public spaces we all use every day, so nobody need feel 'this place isn't for me' and everyone feels welcome.

**Richard Simmons**
**Chief Executive CABE**

# Foreword

Most people now know that disabled people have a right to expect that services provided to the public should be user friendly for disabled people. In many cases the best way to achieve this objective is to ensure that the building is itself accessible. But this immediately raises another question. What exactly is an accessible building? How do building owners and tenants ensure their building is accessible? Is it just about meeting the needs of wheelchair users or is there a wider range of disabled people, such as those who are blind or deaf who also need to be accommodated?

This book provides practical advice on what to do. If design is good for disabled people it will be better for everyone. Equally, some consultants who advise on access have a temptation to gold plate what is necessary. The Disability Discrimination Act requires reasonable adjustments and, by definition, does not require unreasonable adjustments. It is therefore important to understand how much can be done on budgets which might well be limited. Again, helpful advice is provided. It need not cost much. Simple coloured tape can increase the visibility of glass doors and walls. A kick plate not only makes it easier for a wheelchair user to push through a door but it also protects the door and quickly pays for itself.

I welcome this guidance which should enable people to understand access requirements and to undertake access audits. From December 2006 many public bodies will be subject to the Equality Duty under the provisions of the Disability Discrimination Act 2005. If they involve disabled people in determining their policies they are much more likely to fulfil their duty effectively.

Disabled people now have rights to take legal action against companies and public sector organisations which do not provide access to their services. The law is important but how much better if those organisations simply did it right in the first place so the law did not need to be used. This book should help to do just that.

**Bert Massie CBE**
**Chairman of Disability Rights Commission**

# Acknowledgements

I would like to thank Vin Goodwin, for his advice, opinions and encouragement, the Centre for Accessible Environments for providing me with the opportunity to explore the issues that form the basis of this book, and Keith Bright, whose knowledge and enthusiasm have been invaluable. Thanks also to my family for giving support and inspiration.

**Ann Sawyer**
**July 2006**

My thanks go, as always, to current and past members of the Research Group for Inclusive Environments whose work has contributed to the complex research activities on which many comments made in this book are based.

My personal thanks also go to past and present students on the MSc Inclusive Environments programme at Reading for bringing to the course their unique knowledge and real-life working experiences, and for demonstrating that education truly is a two-way process.

My special thanks go to Ann Sawyer who has worked so hard to bring this second edition to fruition.

**Keith Bright**
**July 2006**

Main photograph on cover, Plate 1, Plate 4 and Fig. 4.54 show Woodlands School, reproduced with kind permission from Investors in the Community.

Photograph of sign on cover, Plates 3, 7 and 8 and Fig. 4.63 show Idea Store Whitechapel, reproduced with kind permission from London Borough of Tower Hamlets.

# Introduction

Buildings are designed for people to use – to give shelter, to house, for work and for play. An environment that is designed to be accessible, or inclusive, allows those activities to take place without restricting access to people with certain abilities only. Inclusive design does not disable the users; it enables independent and equal use.

For many owners, designers and managers of buildings and environments, meeting the needs of all users, and especially disabled people, can seem difficult. However, it is possible to address the needs of the great majority of users with design and management solutions that neither conflict with each other, nor are expensive or difficult to carry out. An inclusive approach requires designers and building managers to consider abilities rather than disabilities, and integrate a range of needs into one solution that can be used by everyone. The improvement in accessibility that can result from this approach will benefit all users of the built environment, not just disabled people.

## Inclusive design

Design guidance is often based on the needs of a notional 'average' person; however, everyone varies from the average in some way. People differ in height, strength and dexterity. People have different visual and hearing abilities or may have respiratory impairments or reduced stamina. Some of these people will consider themselves 'disabled', some will not. Some will see their abilities as a natural result of ageing or maybe a temporary illness. Older people may have limited mobility; some may use wheelchairs, sticks or crutches. These and other aids such as spectacles and hearing aids will allow people to alter their abilities. Mobility may be affected by having to carry a child or heavy shopping bags or push a buggy. These are all usual, everyday capacities that should be catered for when designing buildings and environments. An inclusive approach accepts that people have a range of needs and leads to designs that allow the majority of people to use the built environment independently, safely and comfortably.

An example of this would be good, clear, effective signage, efficiently and sensibly used. This is not just needed by people with visual impairments; it is important for everyone and critical for those who are deaf or hard of hearing, people with learning difficulties or disabilities, older people or people whose first language is not that of the information given on the sign. Also, level, firm surfaces, which benefit wheelchair users, will help parents with pushchairs, people using walking aids or those carrying luggage.

An inclusive approach to design and management does not deny that there are specific areas where particular assistance can be provided. Hearing enhancement systems, such as induction loops, or the provision of information in Braille are useful to certain building users. Specific provisions that meet particular needs are also part of inclusive design.

## Principles of universal design

There are many different terms in use to describe inclusive design. Terms such as accessible, trans-generational, or universal all have similar and overlapping definitions; what they all have in common is that the needs of as many people as possible are considered, including parents with children, elderly people and disabled people. The Centre for Universal Design has produced a useful list of principles of universal design that can be applied to products and buildings (see boxed text).

## Costs and benefits

It is often thought that addressing the needs of everyone in new or existing buildings will lead to increased costs. However, careful consideration of the issues at design stage and good management throughout the life of a building can provide and maintain accessible environments at little or no extra cost. Designing buildings

---

**1.1  Principles of universal design**

1  Equitable – the design should be usable by people with diverse abilities and should appeal to all users.
2  Flexible – the design should cater for a wide range of individual preferences and abilities. This may mean some choice in methods of use (such as right or left handed access).
3  Simple and intuitive – use of the design should be easy to understand, regardless of experience, knowledge, language skills, or current concentration level.
4  Perceptible – the design communicates necessary information effectively to the user, regardless of ambient conditions or the user's sensory abilities.
5  Tolerance for error – the design minimises hazards and the adverse consequences of accidental or unintended actions.
6  Low physical effort – the design can be used efficiently and comfortably with a minimum of fatigue.
7  Size and space for approach and use – appropriate size and space is provided for approach, reach, manipulation and use, regardless of user's body size, posture or mobility.

---

and environments to be inclusive from the outset can also avoid the need for costly, and often unsightly, alterations later on.

Elements of the built environment, such as buildings, pedestrian areas and transport infrastructure, are with us for a long time, but their life is dynamic, not static, and there are often opportunities to improve accessibility. Linking improvements to maintenance or refurbishment programmes can help ensure that the work is done cost-effectively.

There are also financial benefits to be had from designing inclusively. The population is ageing; current estimates suggest that by 2015 nearly one in five of us will be over 65. Older people with higher disposable incomes are becoming a more important force in the market place, and with increased opportunities in employment, the spending power of disabled people will also grow. Service providers can increase and broaden their customer base by making their services, and the buildings that house them, accessible to everyone. Employers can benefit from the skills and abilities of disabled people, by ensuring that their buildings and procedures are accessible.

## Disability Discrimination Act 1995

With the introduction of the Disability Discrimination Act 1995 (DDA) the consideration of issues such as access and inclusive design has become even more important. The Act gives rights to disabled people with the intention of eliminating discrimination in the areas of:

- recruitment and employment;
- access to goods, facilities and services;
- buying or renting of land or property;
- education.

Since its introduction, the Act has been amended by the Special Educational Needs and Disability Act 2001 (SENDA), by the Disability Discrimination Act 1995 (Amendment) Regulations 2003, which made extensive changes to the employment and occupation provisions, and most recently by the Disability Discrimination Act 2005.

The DDA applies to the whole of the UK and places duties on employers and service providers not to discriminate against disabled people. The DDA extends the definition of disability to cover a wide range of people including people with hearing and visual impairments, learning difficulties, mental illness and ambulant disabled people, such as those using walking aids or with arthritis. This definition may well be altered over time as cases come before the courts and as other legislation, such as the Human Rights Act, which expands the definition of disability even further, start to have an influence.

The DDA does not directly require buildings to be accessible to all disabled people and does not include standards for accessible building design; it is the services on offer within buildings that are the concern of the Act. However, it is critical that building owners and managers, facilities managers and those commissioning or designing new buildings or works to existing buildings consider the implications of the Act in relation to building design and use. This will involve anticipating the needs of all building users, some of whom will fit the definition of disabled under the Act, and designing and managing buildings accordingly. Knowledge of access audits and access management will be a crucial factor in determining how well this can be done and will allow an effective response to the new legal requirements.

## British Standards and Building Regulations

The publication of BS 8300:2001 Design of buildings and their approaches to meet the needs of disabled people – Code of Practice, and the subsequent revision of Part M of the Building Regulations in 2004, raised standards of good practice in inclusive design.

BS 8300:2001, which was amended in June 2005, gives detailed guidance on the design of domestic and non-domestic buildings. The guidance draws on research, commissioned by the Department of the Environment, Transport and the Regions in 1997 and 2001, into the access needs of disabled people. The research looked into ergonomic issues such as reach ranges and space requirements in order to assess the capabilities and needs of people in relation to the use of buildings.

The BS is the most comprehensive standard to date covering the environmental needs of disabled people and it is likely to be used as a benchmark when considering what is 'reasonable provision' in relation to the Disability Discrimination Act.

The 2004 edition Approved Document M, which gives guidance on the requirements of Part M of the Building Regulations, refers to new and existing buildings being accessible and usable by people, including parents with children, elderly people and disabled people. The dimensional criteria in this edition of Approved Document M have been updated and revised to take account of the guidance given in BS 8300:2001.

The standards and dimensions recommended in this book are generally in line with BS 8300:2001, as amended. The good practice guidance draws on other sources from this country and abroad, from user groups and from the wide experience of the authors.

## Objectives of the manual

The manual covers the design, improvement, maintenance and management of accessible environments. The intention is to encourage designers, owners and managers of buildings to look at how they can provide and operate buildings, services and employment facilities in a way that allows independent and convenient use by everyone.

The manual is intended to enable people with responsibility for the design and management of the built environment to:

- be aware the issues involved in accessibility;
- understand and commission access audits;
- create and manage an access improvement programme;
- maintain accessibility in buildings and working practices; and
- respond effectively to the legal requirements of the Disability Discrimination Act 1995, as amended.

The section covering access auditing gives information on why audits and appraisals should be carried out, explains the audit process and how it fits into an access improvement programme. The section on access management covers the implementation of improvements and the importance of ongoing access management to ensure accessibility is sustained in use.

The manual also gives guidance on handover and commissioning of new and improved buildings, feedback procedures, post-occupancy evaluation and ongoing management of the accessible environment. Relevant legislation and standards are described, explaining the effect on accessible design and giving information on duties and obligations.

The design criteria cover access to and use of buildings and take account of the needs of a wide range of users. The design guidance can be used when designing new buildings or taken as a standard to assess and improve existing ones.

Appendix A contains a number of sheets of 'general acceptability criteria', which can be used to highlight where access problems exist. Appendix B gives sources of reference and further information. Extracts from sample audit reports and access statements are available on the Blackwell website at www.blackwellpublishing. com/theaccessmanual and illustrate various report formats and content. Throughout the manual there are boxes giving hints and tips. The information given in the boxes covers issues that are not always found in standards, legislation or other guidance, and includes advice and thoughts that come from the authors' experience.

Inclusive design is about people and their needs, and, in the context of this manual, how these relate to the design, use and management of the built environment. The manual includes comprehensive information on standards, legislation and good practice, but also recognises that to achieve a truly accessible environment designers and operators of buildings must move beyond compliance with standards and adopt a new way of thinking. Taking a creative approach, considering the needs of everyone, integrating those needs into good, thoughtful designs and practices will help achieve an accessible, inclusive, built environment that enables people to participate fully in all aspects of society.

# Access audits and appraisals

## Introduction

The purpose of an access audit is to establish how well a particular building or environment performs in terms of access and ease of use by a wide range of potential users, including disabled people, and to recommend access improvements. The process involves a thorough site inspection, an assessment of the management and use of the building or environment and the preparation of a report that identifies accessible user-friendly features as well as access problems. The report should recommend access improvements, prioritise action and indicate where improvements can be made through the building's maintenance programme and by altering management procedures. The audit is the first part of the access improvement process and should be followed by the preparation of an access plan setting out the strategy for the implementation of the proposals, and leading to ongoing management of the accessible environment. This will enable building owners to plan ahead for costly improvements and allow alterations to be made cost effectively and over time.

Usually, an audit will consider the needs of all users, and potential users, of a building or environment and assess the factors affecting independent use and access to services. However, an audit may be carried out in response to a particular issue, such as how to meet the needs of a disabled employee in the workplace, and this may affect the scope of the audit and the standards used in assessing accessibility.

It is important to involve the building owners, managers and operators, as appropriate, in the audit process. Many of the issues that arise will be concerned with the operation and management of an environment, not just the fabric.

The term access appraisal is used to describe an audit of the proposals for a development. This involves making a detailed assessment of the proposed level of accessibility in a building or environment using drawings, specifications and consultation with the architect or designer. To be most effective an appraisal should be ongoing throughout the design process.

An audit can also be carried out to assess service provision. This may be useful for an organisation that is defined as a service provider by Part 3 of the Disability Discrimination Act 1995 (DDA) or that wishes to improve its services generally.

## Why carry out an access audit?

An access audit will give a picture of the level of accessibility in a building, identify points of good or bad access, identify areas of need that are not catered for and is a first step in the process of improving accessibility.

---

The increase in accessibility that can result from an access audit and subsequent access improvements will benefit all users of the building. Issues such as poor signs, doors that are heavy to open, and lack of handrails affect everyone, not just disabled people.

---

The reasons for carrying out or commissioning audits and appraisals may include:

- Disability Discrimination Act 1995;
- funding conditions – Lottery funds, grant from trust or other body with specific access requirements;
- to gather data on buildings for comparison or analysis;

- to check compliance with certain standards, such as Part M of the Building Regulations;
- company policy on equal opportunities;
- public relations/company image;
- conservation by use of historic buildings;
- pressure from lobby groups;
- awareness of a particular problem.

The Code of Practice relating to Part 3 of the DDA clearly suggests that service providers are more likely to be able to comply with their duty to make adjustments in relation to physical features if they arrange for an access audit of their premises to be conducted and draw up an access plan or strategy. It states that 'acting on the results of such an evaluation may reduce the likelihood of legal claims against the service provider' (DRC 2002).

**Figure 1.1** A good level of accessibility can benefit a wide range of people, including disabled people.

## Audit preparation

Information about the building, the occupier, the services provided, the length of time the building will be occupied, the available budget and future plans for alterations or refurbishment should be collected before the actual audit commences. Taking all these factors into account will help ensure that the audit covers all the necessary issues and that the recommendations made are relevant, practical and likely to be effective.

Information on the commissioning and the scope of the audit should also be confirmed prior to commencement.

## Information about the building

The size, number and location of buildings should be confirmed, along with their age and type and use. There will be particular issues relevant to specific building types, for example, an education building may have lecture theatres or laboratories with particular requirements, and a theatre will have particular acoustic requirements. The location of public transport and car parking should also be considered.

**Historic buildings**   Whether a building is of any special architectural or historic interest is also relevant, especially if it is listed or there are restrictions on alterations. It should not be assumed that listed buildings cannot be altered. Guidance issued by English Heritage 'Easy Access to Historic Buildings' (EH 2004) acknowledges that in most cases the needs of access and conservation can be reconciled. The guidance quotes Planning Policy Guidance Note 15: Planning and the Historic Environment, which states:

> 'It is important in principle that disabled people should have dignified easy access to and within historic buildings. If it is treated as part of an integrated review of access requirements for all visitors or users, and a flexible and pragmatic approach is taken, it should normally be possible to plan suitable access for disabled people without compromising a building's special interest.'

When considering alterations to an historic or listed building, it is important to establish the extent of the listing. In some buildings, it may be only particular features, such as a façade or staircase, that are listed and alterations may be possible to other parts of the building. Some alterations may be possible even to listed parts if no permanent damage is done to the historic fabric. For example, it may be possible to fit a wheelchair stair lift as long as it can be removed at a later date with no damage to the fabric having occurred. Consultation with the local planning or historic buildings officer is always a good idea.

Even if physical alterations are not possible, there may be other ways of getting around an inaccessible feature, or providing the service or employment opportunity being offered within the building by a 'reasonable alternative method'.

**Figure 1.2** Access to historic buildings can be improved with sensitive, well-designed alterations.

**Future plans**   The length of future occupancy may influence proposals for improvement; whether the building is owned or let is also relevant. Plans for refurbishment or alterations should be taken into account as they may affect access or they may present an opportunity to make access improvements.

## Information about staff, management and building use

It is essential to have information about the occupier and the nature of his or her business, for example, whether the occupier is an organisation that offers, or could offer, a service to members of the public. How a building or environment is used and managed can have a huge impact on its accessibility. A well-designed, accessible building can be made difficult or impossible to use unless management and maintenance procedures take account of access issues. Information on policies, procedures and building use should be collected and relevant issues identified.

Contact with staff, including any employees or other building users who are disabled, will give an opportunity to discuss how the building is used and whether there are any specific access problems. Questions to be asked could include:

- Have staff or management had any access training, or is any planned?
- Is there a member of staff in the company with responsibility for access issues?
- Is there a human resources department or a health and safety section in the company?

## Costs and benefits

In some cases the available budget for improvements to the building may also be relevant as this can affect the scope of any alterations that may be recommended. For example, if the size of the budget prevents the installation of a lift, this may well affect the recommendations for using an upper floor for providing a service or as a place of employment for a current or potential disabled employee.

In certain situations, an employer may be able to obtain grants under schemes such as 'Access to Work', which may affect the extent to which the employer can carry out physical alterations to a building or the provision of facilities for an employee. Knowledge of such schemes and other potential sources of funding are an important part of the service offered by an access auditor or access consultant.

VAT should also be considered. At the time of writing some goods and services can be zero-rated when supplied to charities or for the use of specific disabled people in private residences. It should be made clear whether or not VAT and other costs, such as fees, are included in cost advice given as part of an audit.

The most expensive access improvements may not benefit the greatest numbers of people. Often smaller alterations will have a more wide-ranging effect.

## Access information

The scope of the report and the standards against which access will be assessed should be confirmed prior to the audit. Matters that should be checked include the following:

- the standard against which the building is to be assessed;
- whether the needs of staff are to be considered as well as customers and visitors;
- the access policy of the organisation;
- particular access problems in the building to be audited.

It can be useful to check whether there has been previous contact with an access group, or an access officer, and whether an access audit has been carried out in the past.

Egress, especially in an emergency, is a critical part of the accessibility of a building and is usually affected by both the design of the building and how it is managed. If emergency egress is to be considered, both these issues will need to be audited; if it is not included, this must be made clear to ensure no misunderstandings occur as to the extent of the audit.

## Commissioning

Information concerning the commissioning of the audit is also critical. Instructions covering fees, timescale and scope should be confirmed in writing. Issues of confidentiality should be discussed, together with determining whether or not photographs can be taken during the audit and whether the auditor needs to be accompanied around the building. Wherever possible, copies of floor plans of the building being audited should be obtained as well as copies of visitor information and publicity material.

> In larger commercial and public buildings, floor plans may be displayed alongside fire certificates. These can give an indication of the size and layout of the building.

It is useful to consider whom the report is for and how the information will be used. If the audit information is to be transferred to an internal maintenance or improvement programme, the use of compatible formats or software when collecting the information will assist this process.

> Photographs should be included in the report and can also be a valuable record for the auditor. Factors affecting accessibility, such as lighting, signage or obstructions on circulation routes, can change on a daily basis. It is important to have some record of the level of accessibility at the time of the audit, if only to be used if a dispute arises at a later date.

## How environments are used

It is important to consider the ways in which each area of a building or environment is used, managed and operated rather than just relying on the generic title to describe the function. A building such as a shopping centre or hospital will contain many areas with different functions, where the physical design and type of use of each area may affect the access requirements. For example, within a hospital, the factors affecting accessibility will vary considerably across circulation routes, refreshment areas, wards, operating theatres, waiting rooms and consulting rooms. Some areas will be used by members of the public who are unfamiliar with the building and whose individual needs will be unknown, whilst other areas will be occupied by staff whose needs can be assessed and met. In some buildings visitors may have to rely upon signs for information, in others there may be reception desks where staff are able to identify particular user needs and offer assistance where required. Access may be restricted to some parts of buildings, whereas other areas may be open to everyone.

Entire buildings or parts of buildings can be classified according to use and this approach can be helpful in understanding how to provide services in a non-discriminatory way and how to improve accessibility in ways that will suit the needs of all users.

**Use classification**    There are four use classifications described here:

- use classification 1 – complete freedom of movement;
- use classification 2 – controlled entry/freedom of movement;
- use classification 3 – free entry/controlled movement;
- use classification 4 – controlled entry/controlled movement.

**Use classification 1 – complete freedom of movement**    A building or area in this classification would be one where the user or visitor is free to enter, wander around, probably in no particular sequence, and leave without the need to make any contact with potential assistance points such as a reception/information desk or security point. Environments that fall into this category may include shops and shopping centres, department stores, supermarkets, some hospitals and non-fee paying museums and exhibitions.

> An environment in this use classification is likely to contain long travel distances. The provision of seating, preferably where visitors do not have to pay to sit down as in a café, will be helpful to many people, especially older people and disabled people.

In environments that allow users complete freedom of movement, information will need to be provided remotely, usually by signs. The provision of an information point or help desk may assist some visitors but will not remove the need to provide information remotely, as it cannot be assumed that all visitors will make use of it.

Environments that allow the type of freedom of movement described here are likely to be the most difficult to design and manage to ensure appropriate levels of accessibility for all users. There may be a wide range of needs to be met and little opportunity to provide specific assistance. In such environments the provision of good environmental services (lighting, acoustics, visual contrast, etc.), appropriate communication facilities (signs, audible and visual information systems, etc.) and ongoing staff training are essential.

**Figure 1.3** Good, clear signs are necessary where there is freedom of movement.

> Many people, but especially older people and those with hearing impairments, dislike environments with poor acoustical qualities, or ones that contain equipment with loud background noises.

**Use classification 2 – controlled entry/freedom of movement**
Environments in this category will have some point of control, usually a payment desk or security point, but, after passing that point, users will be allowed the type of free, usually unrestricted, movement described above. This category might include sports halls, ice rinks, fee-paying museums and art galleries, some hospitals, exhibition halls, libraries, some educational buildings, some hotels and some offices.

> Good lighting is essential at any reception desk or information desk to ensure that people with sensory impairments are able to communicate effectively. However, it is not just more lighting that is needed, it is appropriately designed lighting that maximises visibility without increasing glare or shadows.

In such environments there is still a need to deliver information and assistance remotely once the visitor has passed the point of control, but there is also the opportunity, if management practices are appropriate, for particular user needs to be identified and for assistance to be offered. It is important to consider the potential needs of visitors, have the ability to provide appropriate assistance if required, and have contingency plans in place for those situations which are more difficult to foresee.

**Use classification 3 – free entry/controlled movement**   This type of environment will usually have a central entrance through which the visitors enter, but once inside, movement around the building will be restricted. Examples of this type of classification include town halls, civic centres, major post offices, law courts, airports, bus and railway stations, some hospitals, theatres, cinemas, some multi-tenanted offices, restaurants, banks (as a customer) and some hotels.

Some larger buildings may have areas of controlled movement combined with other areas where there is complete freedom of movement. An example is a hospital where there may be complete freedom of movement around the refreshment areas, shops and corridors, and controlled entry to wards and clinics. The methods of providing information may vary according to the type of use.

**Use classification 4 – controlled entry/controlled movement**   In this type of environment, security will usually be a major issue and the type of visitor will be restricted. Controlling the entry to an environment allows an assessment of the needs of all users to be made at the initial point of contact, providing that that initial means of requesting entry to the environment is, itself, fully accessible.

Examples of this type of classification would include offices with car park controls or entry phones/CCTV, some schools, some multi-tenanted offices, research laboratories, and some banks (as a customer or an employee). In buildings of this type, management issues will be of great importance. Consideration should also be given to how the building will actually function during all the time it is in use. For example, a school may fit into this classification during the day but may have complete freedom of movement in the evening if it is being used for evening classes or community projects.

---

Signs provided in schools should be clear and simple and designed to meet the needs of the children using the building during the day, but also the adults who may use the building in the evening.

---

An analysis of a building using this system of classification can help to give a more accurate picture of the specific access requirements of each individual area and can highlight opportunities for improvements.

## Who uses the environment?

It is also important to consider who uses the environment being audited and how this may affect general and specific recommendations to improve accessibility. A service provider has to anticipate the needs of his or her customers, but an employer can identify the needs of his or her workforce, though not those of potential employees. Whether or not specific access requirements can be identified will affect the advice given in an audit.

For example, an employee may require a greater amount of circulation space at a workspace, a particular desk arrangement or the provision of special equipment. These measures will be identified in relation to a current or future employee and so can be carried out when the need arises. In addition to recommendations aimed at achieving a good overall standard of accessibility, an audit report should recommend that procedures are in place to deal with potential future needs that cannot be identified in advance, and identify issues that are not currently causing problems but may need to be dealt with in the future.

Recommendations to alter storage arrangements in a workplace to accommodate reach from a wheelchair may not be necessary where there are no wheelchair users using the storage facilities. However, the access audit could raise the issue and note that alterations should be made when the need arises.

## Who should carry out an access audit?

To carry out an audit successfully the auditor or consultant needs to have two main areas of knowledge:

- a comprehensive knowledge of the needs of disabled people in order to identify and understand the difficulties caused by the built environment;

- a working knowledge of building constructio
  knowledge of design to be able to identify pract
  appropriate solutions.

> An auditor does not require the ability to produce detailed
> designs, though some may have this skill. An audit will
> usually stop short of design solutions, though may include
> sketches showing, for example, how a change of level could
> be overcome with a lift or ramp.

Also helpful are skills in surveying, assessing and communicating views and opinions, especially in report format.

There is a view that an access auditor should be a disabled person, as only then will he or she have first-hand knowledge of the needs of disabled people. Others say that disabled people are individuals and it should not be assumed that they will have an in-depth knowledge of the access needs of others. All disabled people are likely to have experienced problems with the built environment, and this may lead to an awareness of access issues, but a wheelchair user will not necessarily be aware of the specific needs of a person with a visual or hearing impairment or vice versa.

However, it is clearly desirable to involve disabled people in the audit process and this can be done in various ways. Where there is a local access group, members could be invited to contribute to the audit process. Members of staff who are disabled must be consulted as they will be aware of access issues in the building and also may have particular access needs. On larger projects it may be possible to set up a focus group or committee of people representing different interests to provide input into the audit or appraisal process.

> If an access group is involved or if individual disabled people
> are invited to join a focus group it will be necessary to allow
> for additional costs incurred. It should never be assumed that
> people would contribute their expertise without payment.

place when a building is occupied, as this
o observe procedures and assess the building
busy at certain periods of the day, or perhaps
purpose in the evening, the audit should
f this use also.
nd the weather may affect any observations
in the report. Comments on glare, visual con-
trast and general illumination of the environment will relate pre-
cisely to conditions at the time of the audit and these may vary from
day to day or even from hour to hour. In addition, the presence of
rain, leaves, snow and ice can also affect the safety of external
routes and raise issues of maintenance. Just because certain factors
are not present at the time of the audit does not mean their influence on the accessibility of an environment can be ignored.

Always think about solutions while auditing. It is often easier
to identify a possible solution when in the building actually
looking at the problem.

## What to audit

The audit should cover both physical features and issues of management and use.
Physical features usually include:

- **external environment** – including approach, parking, transport
  links, routes, street furniture and external ramps and steps;
- **entrance** – including visibility, entry controls, doors, thresholds
  and lobbies;
- **reception area** – including layout, reception desk, waiting area,
  signs, visual and acoustic factors;
- **horizontal circulation** – including ease of navigation, corridors,
  doors, directional information, internal surfaces;

- **vertical circulation** – including internal steps and stairs, ramps, escalators and lifts;
- **WCs** – general provision, WCs for ambulant disabled people, accessible WCs and baby changing facilities;
- **specific facilities** – such as changing areas, bathrooms and showers, bedrooms, storage, refreshment areas, service desks, waiting areas and assembly areas;
- **controls and equipment** – coin and card operated devices, building services controls, window controls, alarms, entry phones;
- **communication systems** – such as telephones/text phones, lift voice announcers and audiovisual displays;
- **emergency egress** – including escape routes, refuges, alarms, fire protected lifts, emergency lighting;
- **signs and way finding** – including overall layout of building, sign type and location, use of landmark features, maps and guides, visual contrast, audible features and olfactory features;
- **lighting** – general and workplace;
- **acoustic environment** – including background noise, hearing enhancement systems, acoustic conditions suitable for intended use.

It is not just the physical features of a building or environment that affect accessibility. Access to information, staff attitudes and working practices can have a major impact on actual and perceived accessibility and can also sometimes provide the easiest and most cost-effective ways to improve accessibility.

For many disabled people, access to information is as important as physical access. The availability of publicity and information material is essential to allow disabled people to participate, contribute and make planned use of services. Information should be provided in a variety of formats to be appropriate to people's needs. Staff should be properly trained to be aware of the needs of disabled people and to manage the environment and the services in a way that allows equal access to all users.

The audit should consider how such matters are dealt with and include information on:

- **access to information** – publicity and information material, formats available, text phones, hearing enhancement;
- **attitudes of staff and management** – training in disability and accessibility issues;
- **management practices, policies and procedures** – including those relating to emergency egress;
- **maintenance issues** – in relationship to achieving or maintaining accessibility;
- **use of the building** – the way in which the building or environment is used by employees, visitors and members of the public.

To give a comprehensive assessment of the level of accessibility and to identify the opportunities for improvement an audit must take account of these issues.

> Access improvements can often be made at no cost by increasing awareness and altering policies and procedures.

## Assessment standards and dimensions

The standard for assessment should be agreed before the audit commences. It might be general good practice, or a particular publication or standard could be identified, such as BS 8300: 2001. The audit should always consider usability, and look at how people move through the environment and use the facilities safely and as independently as possible.

> The skill of the auditor or access consultant is in judging what is reasonable; best practice standards may not be found in existing buildings and may be impossible to achieve.

It is important to take dimensions on site and to be clear what standards are being used. It is unhelpful to note that a feature is adequate if the standard of assessment is not clear. The standards adopted for the audit should be used consistently throughout the building.

The audit should include detailed factual description, with relevant dimensions as appropriate, and fully describe physical features, facilities and management practices.

## Audit equipment

The auditor will need, at the very least, a tape measure and some means of recording the information collected. It is desirable to use, in addition, a camera or video camera and, where appropriate, a door weight measure, a light meter, a sound meter, a gradient measure and a means of testing an induction loop.

Where equipment such as light meters and weight gauges are not available, subjective judgements may have to suffice. It is useful to have these judgements made by people who will be most affected by the feature being assessed, for example, by asking a wheelchair user's opinion of a deep pile carpet or by taking the advice of a person of reduced strength or mobility on door opening and closing forces.

## General acceptability criteria

Lists of 'general acceptability criteria' are given in Appendix A. These lists, relating to car parking, external areas, entrances, stairs and steps, ramps, lifts, horizontal circulation and accessible WCs, can be used to highlight where access problems exist. The lists should not to be used as a substitute for an audit, but as part of an initial stage to identify where standards fall short of good practice and further investigation is necessary.

## The journey

The audit should take the form of a sequential journey, starting at the point at which people may start their visit to the building, continuing into and around the building, and finishing with safe egress from it. It is useful to separate out some major elements, such as vertical and horizontal circulation, WCs, signs, lighting, auditoria and means of escape, to help structure the audit. Plans of the building can be used to organise a route for the audit, check off the areas visited and annotate with the information collected.

> Standard checklists can be useful, as long as the checklist does not limit the information collected. A tick in a box is very unlikely to give sufficient information to fully describe an issue.

## Recording the information

Information can be recorded using notes, sketches, Dictaphone (or dictation to an assistant), camera, video camera and annotation of existing drawings. If a laptop or palm top computer is used, the information can be put into a predetermined format or onto appropriate software.

> It is useful to record examples of good access as well as access problems. Issues not covered in design guidance may arise on site or from discussions with staff and new good practice may be learnt.

## Audits of services

The concept of the service audit has come into being largely because of the DDA. The Act is concerned primarily with employment and the provision of services, not the design of buildings. When assessing an environment to see if the requirements of Part 3 of the DDA are met, it is the provision of services that is the critical issue. A service audit differs from an access audit as the focus of the process is on customer service, rather than the built environment and the effect it has on the provision of services.

The assessment is of the services that are provided by an organisation to its clientele and, in relation to the DDA, the aim would be to identify any areas of service provision that are discriminatory. The measurements taken are of service provision, attitudes, training, etc., and the information is gathered from staff and recipients of the service.

The methods used to gather information can include assessment of staff education and training, staff motivation and commitment and customer and staff feedback. Face-to-face interviews with staff and customers, focus groups, telephone interviews, written questionnaires and mystery shopper techniques can also be used. Information is collected and analysed and used to produce an objective assessment of the level of service provided, highlighting opportunities for improvement.

As with an access audit, there is a need to set out assessment criteria, identify good service and make recommendations for improvements, with costs and priorities where appropriate.

**Figure 1.4** A ramp may be provided as a short-term solution while awaiting a major refurbishment of the building.

# The report

## Preparing the report

In preparing an audit report, it is essential to consider the purpose of the audit and for whom it is designed. It is critical that the information is presented in a way that will allow the building manager or owner to make best use of it. The audit report, and its format, should encourage, not hinder, implementation of the proposed improvements.

The purpose of the report is:

- to record the current access situation in the building or environment;
- to explain how the building or environment can best cater for the needs of all its users;
- to set out priorities and procedures for carrying out the recommended improvements;
- to identify the availability of resources, where appropriate;
- to set out how accessibility can be sustained in use.

The report should describe the building or environment and the current access situation, recommend access improvements, prioritise action, give costs and indicate where improvements can be made through a maintenance programme or by management action.

Information can be presented using:

- the narrative method, with a description of the existing situation and identification of the problem, followed by a recommendation for remedial action;
- the tabular method, where as much information as possible is given in tables with a minimum of text;
- a combination of both, such as a narrative format with a tabular summary.

See Blackwell website, www.blackwellpublishing.com/theaccessmanual for examples of audits and possible formats.

However, whichever format is used, a standard report should always include the following:

- an introduction describing the function of the building, and how the building is currently being used, and noting any particular access problems;
- a detailed description of the existing access situation, with dimensional information and considering each identified element of the audit in turn;
- recommendations for improvement, using a stated standard or standards;
- priority ratings for the recommended improvements;
- cost information where required;
- a summary, identifying the main points of the report.

A report should include photographs and plans of the building, and sources of further information where required. It can be useful, particularly where there are a number of buildings being assessed, to include a manual of design guidance as an appendix to the report.

## Description of current situation

There should be detailed information collected and presented describing the elements of the building and current access arrangements. It is not sufficient to state that an element is inadequate or incorrect; dimensions should be given with a detailed description.

It is also helpful to note points of good access, not just elements that fall below a certain standard.

---

Audits which only highlight or identify problems can be very demoralising.

Wherever possible, highlight some areas of good practice, if only to ensure that the service provider or employer does not simply give up and do nothing!

# Recommendations

Recommendations should explain how a feature could be altered or removed to improve access. Recommendations will cover many areas and not all will require alterations to the building. There may be a management procedure that could be improved, such as better policing of disabled parking bays.

Many issues will be able to be dealt with as part of a regular maintenance programme; the introduction of visual contrast in redecorations is an example. Relocating a service or facility to another building could also solve an access problem.

Refurbishment of a building may give opportunities to make access improvements such as altering door widths or automating door opening. It may also be possible to adjust floor levels or incorporate ramps.

# Priority rating

It is useful to prioritise recommendations. An example of a rating system is as follows:

(1)  implement immediately to eliminate a severe barrier or a hazard to access to and use of the building by disabled staff or visitors, including potential health and safety or occupier liability issues;
(2)  implement as soon as practicable to improve access;
(3)  plan action to be implemented when relevant area/element of building is refurbished/upgraded;
(4)  plan adaptation to be part of a workplace assessment to be implemented to suit the needs of an identified member of staff;
(M)  implement and regularly review as part of specific or regular maintenance or renewal;
(A)  no action is reasonably practicable. Arrange for assistance to be readily available or for the service or employment opportunity to be provided by an appropriate and reasonable alternative means.

The rating given to recommendations will depend upon a number of factors and may vary from project to project. It may also vary for identical access solutions for different service providers or employers. Improvement to accessibility will be a major factor, but priority may also be influenced by the availability of funds for certain types of work, proposed works to the building or length of future occupancy. A method for setting priorities must be agreed in advance of the audit.

## Costings

Information on the cost of the recommended improvements is a useful element of an access audit report. The source of the cost information, such as the 'Access Audit Price Guide' (BCIS 2002), should also be given.

In many cases it will not be possible to provide accurate and detailed costings unless the recommended improvements are taken to detailed design stage. However, it will usually be possible to provide broad band cost information.

Recommendations can be categorised as low, medium or high cost or cost bands can be given, say:

- up to £1000;
- £1000 to £10 000;
- £10 000 to £25 000;
- over £25 000.

The range of each band will depend, to some degree, upon the type of recommendations and the overall budget.

---

As with all other maintenance or improvement work, the costs will vary according to many factors, such as whether in-house staff or contract staff are used to undertake the work.

Always establish this before offering cost bands or clearly identify the grounds on which costs have been developed.

## Summary

An executive summary is a useful device and gives the opportunity to set out the main points in a report succinctly. The summary can provide a picture of the current access situation in a building and identify the key issues in the report.

> Often the summary will be the first part of the report that is read, if an overview of the issues is sought. Too much care cannot be taken to ensure that the summary is well constructed, concise and accurate.

The summary should also draw attention to issues of building operation and procedure and set out how the audit fits in to the access improvement process. It is critical that the audit is seen in context and as the first part of a process, not the conclusion.

## Access appraisals

An access appraisal is an assessment of the access provision in proposals for a new development, refurbishment or alteration. Appraisals can also be used to assess access policies, access briefs, publicity and information material and maintenance programmes. Appraisals are carried out for many of the same reasons as audits, and the information that should be gathered beforehand is similar.

When looking at proposals for buildings and environments the appraisal follows the pattern of an audit, but the journey is taken on paper and in discussions, rather than through the building. Potential access problems can be identified or anticipated; however, a comprehensive review depends on there being a sufficient level of detail and information available. Physical features should be assessed, as in an audit, but the guidance given should also include issues of management and use.

Recommendations for access improvements should be given, though in some cases these may not be as prescriptive as when carrying out an access audit. The appraisal may suggest that a particular layout or feature will make access difficult and recommend that an area be redesigned bearing in mind certain factors. Usually, an appraisal will not include detailed redesign of a proposal, but will provide the necessary information to allow the designer to improve the proposed accessibility. It is preferable that the auditor or access consultant is involved in a project through all stages of design, construction and commissioning.

## Information available

The level of information provided in proposals will vary depending on the stage the design process has reached and this will affect the guidance that can be given. Often detailed information will not be available when the appraisal is carried out and requests should be made for further detail. As well as looking at plans of the proposals, specifications and schedules should be checked. Inevitably there will be some areas where no information is available, but detailed recommendations can still be provided to ensure that issues are picked up at the appropriate time. An access appraisal report can become a checklist for a designer to use as the design develops, to ensure that all the relevant areas are covered.

## The report

An access appraisal report can have a similar format to an audit report, listing current features and making recommendations for access improvements. It may not be appropriate to include priorities and costings, if the appraisal is carried out at design stage. However, as an appraisal is usually not a static exercise, as the design will be evolving during the appraisal process, it may be more appropriate for the appraisal to take the form of a series of 'plan checks'. These can be carried out at various stages and make recommendations that can be 'ticked off' once implemented.

## Ongoing involvement of auditor

If an appraisal is requested for a funding or grant submission, it may take place at an early stage in the design process and the involvement of the auditor may be limited. It is preferable for an auditor to have an ongoing relationship with the designer throughout a project, as this will allow assessment of more detailed proposals and specifications as they become available.

It is becoming more usual for an access consultant to be involved in large projects from the start, as happens with consultants in other fields. This allows the consultant to have input throughout the design and construction process and this level of involvement is likely to result in a more integrated design solution. There should also be a method of passing on access information once the building is commissioned to ensure that accessible features are understood, made use of and not altered unknowingly.

## Building use and management

Issues of building use and management need to be taken into account in an appraisal, as in an audit. Information relating to these issues should be included in any report and areas where use and management may influence access should be highlighted.

## Skills required

Skills in reading and understanding plans are required to carry out an access appraisal of proposals using drawings. These include the use of scale, drawing conventions and symbols. There will be a need to translate the information given on the drawings and in the specifications into a three-dimensional picture of the building or environment to be able to anticipate fully any potential access issues.

As with access auditing, a knowledge of the environmental needs of disabled people is required, and a working knowledge of building construction and design.

## Access statements

An access statement provides an opportunity for developers, designers and managers of buildings and environments to demonstrate their commitment to accessibility and to set out and record issues relating to accessibility throughout strategic, design, construction and occupation phases of a project.

In the initial stages of a project an access statement can be used to record the elements of the brief that relate to access. At this strategic level it will be a statement of intent and can demonstrate how the project will meet any relevant legislation. The form of the access statement will depend upon the size, nature and complexity of the project but should contain, where relevant, the following information:

- a brief explanation of the client's policies and approach to access;
- sources of advice and guidance on access which will be followed;
- details of any consultations undertaken or planned;
- an explanation of any specific issues affecting accessibility and details of access solutions adopted, including those which deviate from recognised sources of good practice;
- details of the management and maintenance management policies adopted, or to be adopted, to maintain features enhancing accessibility.

Where good practice cannot or may not be met, the access statement should say why, what the implications are for the users, and what other steps are being taken to lessen any adverse effects on accessibility. When a designer wishes to depart from current guidance, the access statement can be used to explain how a proposed feature will provide an equivalent standard of accessibility.

Consultation with disabled people and other interested groups should be seen as a crucial element in the preparation of an access statement and undertaken as early as possible in the development process.

## Access statements for planning and building regulation applications

As the project progresses, the access statement can develop into a document to be submitted with a planning application. Design and access statements are required to be submitted with most planning applications (see Chapter 3 Planning Legislation and Guidance for further details).

At planning stage information added to the statement should include:

- details of the size, scale and potential uses in the development;
- details of the site plan;
- details of access issues that have been considered in formulating the planning application;
- information on the planning guidance and legislation that has been considered, and the technical guidance which it is proposed will be used to develop the design at detail stage;
- information on public and other transport links with the development and car parking;
- how means of escape will be addressed, if appropriate.

The access statement should then be developed further to include more detailed and technical issues and become a suitable document to submit with a building regulation application. The statement can also be used to identify any areas where the project design deviates from guidance in established sources of good or best practice. It is important to identify the reasons why and, importantly, the design team's justification that the proposed deviation provides an accessibility standard which is the same as, or is an improvement on, the established guidance.

Further information on access statements at planning and building regulation stages is given in Chapter 3.

## Occupancy access plan

This access statement, or access plan, will draw on all of the previous statements to demonstrate a commitment to accessibility and identify how this will be followed through in policies, practices and management. Access plans are considered in detail in Chapter 2.

By developing a document that passes to those who will undertake the long-term management of a facility, the access statement process will assist in ensuring that the evolving duty placed on service providers, employers and educators under the DDA can be better addressed. As a document that captures the good decisions on accessibility made at the design stage, the statement can also help to ensure that those decisions are not lost or reversed by those responsible for the management of the building throughout its life.

Further guidance from the Disability Rights Commission on the suggested content and format of an access statement can be found on their website www.drc-gb.org under Employers and Services.

# 2 Access management

## Introduction

An access audit is the first step in improving the accessibility of a building or environment. On completion of the audit, the access improvement process, to be effective, should continue with the preparation of an access plan. The access plan provides a strategy for the implementation of the improvements, leading to ongoing management of the accessible environment. Active management of the improvement process can help ensure that the work is done cost-effectively, incorporated into existing maintenance procedures or refurbishment programmes where appropriate and will allow planning for future maintenance or management input.

In new projects an access statement, which has grown with the project to incorporate intentions and provisions, can be developed to form the basis of an occupancy access plan. Accessibility does not end with specification, it needs to be sustained in use.

## Ongoing access management

### The access plan

An access plan is a strategy for improving accessibility developed from an access audit and can help ensure that access is an ongoing concern, help identify opportunities for change and is a useful tool for meeting obligations under the DDA.

The Code of Practice relating to Part 3 of the DDA states:

'Service providers are more likely to comply with their duty to make adjustments under the Act if they:

- audit physical and non-physical barriers to access for disabled people;
- make adjustments and put them in place;
- provide training for staff which is relevant to the adjustments;
- draw the adjustments to the attention of disabled people;
- let disabled people know how to request assistance;
- regularly review the effectiveness of adjustments and act on findings of the review.'

An access plan can incorporate the above recommendations and start to ensure that access is an ongoing issue that is included in, for example, planned maintenance programmes. The adoption of a strategic approach will allow access improvements to be made in a sensible and cost-effective way, where major items of expenditure can be identified and budgeted for and other items included in everyday management or maintenance.

The access plan should incorporate:

- a schedule of works that has been devised to take into account the priority and cost information in the audit;
- processes to allow regular updating of the audit information;
- links to maintenance and management procedures.

The plan should set out procedures to ensure that when opportunities for access improvements arise they are recognised and not lost and should identify where maintenance or management input is required to make or sustain access improvements.

## Issues requiring management input

The following management and maintenance issues should be considered to ensure that access is achieved and maintained:

- **car parking** – allocation and management of designated bays;

> It is not sufficient to provide designated car parking bays. There must be an appropriate and effective management procedure in operation to ensure bays are only used by disabled people. If the use of bays is not controlled this may well be seen as a discriminatory management practice.

- **external routes** – keeping in good repair and free of obstructions such as free-standing signs or bicycles chained to railings or ramp handrails, clearing leaves, ice, snow and surface water, trimming vegetation to keep routes clear and signs visible;
- **doors** – adjustment of door closers, ironmongery kept in good working order, pass doors kept unlocked;
- **horizontal circulation** – keeping routes free from obstructions, keeping furniture layouts and seating arrangements accessible, making available auxiliary aids such as temporary ramps;

**Figure 2.1** Obstructions such as these should be identified as problems associated with working practices. Assessing if it is a space problem or a staff training issue should be part of any access audit.

- **vertical circulation** – regular checking of lifts to ensure floor of car aligns with finished floor level, maintenance checks on short rise and wheelchair stair lifts;
- **WCs** – checking manoeuvring space in accessible compartments not obstructed by bins, sanitary disposal equipment, etc., replenishment of toilet paper and paper towels in accessible WCs as well as other WCs, assistance alarm cord hanging free and available for use;
- **communication** – new signs to integrate with existing sign system, no *ad hoc* homemade signs, and all information kept up to date, signers and audio description services provided as necessary, appropriate provision of accurate access information and other literature;
- **hearing enhancement systems** – advertising, regularly checking and maintaining, ensuring loop positions at counters are available to users, staff trained to use equipment;
- **alarm systems** – checking and staff training in response procedures;

> If vibrating personal pagers are used to alert people who are deaf or hard of hearing when the fire alarm is activated, it is essential to ensure that batteries are kept charged, regular maintenance on the pagers is carried out, and that they are compatible with the systems they are linked to – at all times.

- **surfaces** – ensuring cleaning does not cause slippery surfaces, maintaining junctions to avoid worn surfaces becoming tripping hazards, replacing like with like, maintaining visual contrast in redecoration;
- **lighting** – replacing of bulbs, keeping windows and light fittings clean;
- **means of escape** – checking exit routes and refuges for obstructions, staff training, regular practices, maintenance of fittings and equipment, reviewing evacuation procedures for employees and visitors;
- **security** – ensuring security procedures do not conflict with accessibility good practice;
- **training** – ensuring staff training is ongoing and appropriate;
- **health and safety policies** – to include information on access, risk assessment;

- **responsibilities for access** – identifying who is responsible and gives approval for improvements, setting priorities, ensuring access is included in maintenance and refurbishment programmes, arranging temporary relocation of services provided within building where there are access limitations, providing auxiliary aids, providing assistance when required, reviewing numbers of disabled people using a service, establishing and running user groups;
- **funding for access improvements** – identifying specific access funds or grants, funds for specific employees such as 'Access to work', use of the maintenance budget;
- **policy review** – regularly reviewing all policies, practices and procedures affecting access.

There may well be other issues relating to specific buildings types and functions. The access plan should take account of any particular requirements.

## Opportunities for improving accessibility

Within the general maintenance of any building and environment, there are often opportunities to introduce measures that improve accessibility, most of which can be undertaken at little or no extra cost.

For example, throughout the life of most buildings there will be repair and refurbishment carried out, perhaps in response to:

- schedules of dilapidations at the end of a lease;
- work undertaken to meet ongoing health and safety or environmental health requirements, such as redecorating or replacing tiling in toilets and kitchens or upgrading lighting;
- replacement of finishes as part of ongoing repairs and refurbishments, including the renewal of floor finishes or redecoration;
- the replacement of old or broken facilities such as taps, light switches, furniture, toilet flushes and larger items such as lifts;
- change of corporate identity, offering opportunities to improve company information and signs.

**Figure 2.2** Refurbishment can offer opportunities for improving access, such as adding a lift to a change of level.

Alterations and extensions may not be required to be accessible by building regulations, but can afford opportunities for improvement. If external areas are refurbished, there may be opportunities for repaving in different materials to identify routes or adding outdoor seating. Inside the building there may be opportunities for improvements during redecoration programmes to change wall tiles in WCs or introduce new colour schemes to provide contrast. Major alterations may give the chance of levelling out differences in floor levels or providing ramps.

Elements of the built environment, such as buildings, pedestrian areas and transport infrastructure, are with us for a long time – but their life is dynamic, not static. There are often opportunities to improve accessibility for everyone – but there are also a greater number of opportunities to make it worse if all the relevant issues are not fully understood.

## Opportunities to maintain accessibility

The adoption of good management practices such as planned maintenance programmes offers considerable opportunity to address and improve accessibility. The access audit can highlight maintenance issues that affect accessibility, and a planned maintenance programme can ensure that there is a continuing commitment to maintain accessibility where it has been achieved. It can involve regular inspection routines to ensure all aspects of the building are kept up to a good standard of repair and allow planning of expenditure for maintenance of, and implementation of, improvements.

For example, even something as simple as painting nosings onto a staircase where they did not exist previously will require the nosings to be reviewed on a regular basis, and for money to be available to repaint the nosings when required. The installation of induction loops requires an ongoing commitment to maintenance

**Figure 2.3** Once a nosing is painted, a commitment is made to re-inspection, repair or redecoration/replacement. The implications in terms of duties and obligations under the DDA should be considered for all access issues.

and testing; a platform lift may require a rather more expensive maintenance contract.

Issues of maintenance that arise in the access audit should be identified and linked to maintenance programmes to ensure that they are dealt with on an ongoing basis.

---

It is not sufficient to simply provide a facility such as an induction loop. The loop must be operational when the person who needs to use it actually visits the building. If it is not functioning, they could argue that management procedures covering the testing and maintenance of equipment are discriminatory.

A lift that is not working when it is required will discriminate against those who need to use it to access a service or employment opportunity. Lifts can break down and the service provider or employer may be required to answer questions such as:

- What procedures are in place to ensure problems with such an important access facility are dealt with efficiently?

and, if it happens regularly,

- What has been done, in terms of management practices, policies and procedures, to limit the impact of the problem for disabled people?

Good provision is essential – appropriate ongoing management is critical.

---

## Occupying the building

When a new building is occupied, or after improvements have been made to an existing building, there will be a number of opportunities to ensure accessibility is fully achieved and reviewed.

## Handover and commissioning of new or improved buildings

At the handover and commissioning stage of a new development, or after a programme of access improvement works has been carried out, there may be some small alterations and adjustments that will benefit accessibility that were not obvious at design or construction stage. Issues such as the location of signs, or the redirection of lighting to avoid glare, need to be dealt with to ensure that the best possible level of accessibility is achieved. There will also be written procedures to prepare or revise, such as health and safety policies, employment policies and security procedures, all of which should take account of access issues.

## Feedback

Information should be passed back to those responsible for the design or improvement programme on whether certain aspects or improvements are successful. Feedback can prevent faulty details being used again and inform designers, clients and access officers of how their ideas work in practice. A formal system of collecting and using feedback to inform future projects can prevent some very useful information being lost forever. An accessibility review should be carried out on all projects and records kept of improvements and results.

## Post-occupancy evaluation

Post-occupancy evaluations look at such issues as:

- the effectiveness of improvements;
- whether more disabled people are using the building or service;
- whether management is making the most of the improvements;
- whether the improvements have been effectively publicised.

A post-occupancy evaluation gathers information about the use of a building or environment from interviews and focus groups, might include carrying out an access audit after a building is completed or improvements have been made, and will analyse the data collected to give a picture of what works and what does not. The evaluation can give very useful information that can be used in the building studied and to inform future projects.

Even where a full evaluation is not carried out it can be useful to review the access audit recommendations after improvements have been made. There may have been other work carried out at the same time as the improvement work that has created more access problems; things may not have been implemented as originally intended and so might not be effective.

## Information and training

### Building manual

Where there is a manual covering issues related to the day-to-day running of a building, it should include information on the steps taken to achieve and maintain accessibility. If there is not a general building manual, an access manual could be set up.

The manual should include a copy of any access audit together with a record of specific measures taken to achieve or improve access. There should also be a permanent record of the specification of internal finishes, together with some explanatory notes, to ensure that issues of visual contrast are not forgotten when the building is redecorated. Information on maintenance of lifts or induction loops and guidance on good housekeeping, such as cleaning methods to ensure that floors are not made slippery or guidance on keeping corridors free of obstructions, should also be included.

Issues of accessibility should also be included in other relevant sections of any manual, such as those covering health and safety, security and emergency evacuation.

A manual will help to ensure that what has been learned is not lost and that access becomes an ongoing concern.

### Access guide

In some buildings it may not be possible to remove a physical barrier or it may be necessary, because of the nature of the business, to adopt practices and policies that do not allow independent access to a service or employment opportunity. For example, listed building consent may be refused for the installation of permanent ramps or a platform lift, requiring the use of temporary ramps on request; security arrangements appropriate to the service being offered may not allow unaccompanied travel around a building.

If there are unavoidable barriers to physical access which it would not be reasonable to remove, when judged on the merits of each individual case, making that information available in publicity material can allow a disabled person to plan his or her journey or visit and, where possible, enable arrangements to be made to remove or reduce the impact of such barriers.

An access guide, available in alternative formats, can advise all potential users of a service of any physical or managerial issues that might affect their access to the service. The guide can be sent out in advance to allow people to plan their visit, book a parking space or just be aware of areas where the access might be restricted. The information contained in the guide should also be available on a website or telephone information line, where appropriate.

## Training

Staff training is critical to maintain access, to overcome shortcomings in building design and to provide accessible services and employment opportunities. Training can cover areas such as disability awareness and equality, use of equipment such as platform lifts and induction loops, British Sign Language, hearing awareness, clear lip speaking, guiding people with visual impairments and general access awareness.

Where access improvements are made to a building or accessible features incorporated in a new building, it is extremely important that staff understand how these improvements or features work in practice. If staff lack awareness, it is likely that full accessibility will not be achieved, whatever the design of the building.

> The interface between staff and customer is critical. It is here that the effectiveness of any accessibility practices and provisions will be tested, and where the disabled user will judge the reasonableness of any shortcomings in access to the service being offered.

## Publicity

Where a good level of access has been achieved, either in a new building or following access improvements to an existing building, it can be useful to publicise this information. Contacting a local access group or disability organisation, or arranging publicity in a local paper, can encourage people to make use of accessible buildings and services. This, in turn, will encourage the maintenance of the accessible service and help ensure that the benefits of improving accessibility are visible.

# 3 Legislation, regulations and standards

## Introduction

There are many responsibilities placed on designers, managers and owners of buildings by legislation and regulations relating to the accessibility of the built environment. The Building Regulations and the Disability Discrimination Act both have a major influence on accessibility and their requirements should be taken into account in the design and management of buildings and environments. Planning law and planning policy guidance cover issues that may affect access, as does other legislation in areas such as health and safety, occupier liability and fire precautions.

Legislation covering human rights and equal opportunities also influences the need for accessible environments. The Human Rights Act 1998 incorporates into UK law rights and freedoms guaranteed by the European Convention on Human Rights, and the Equal Treatment Directive covers access to employment and training.

BS 8300, which was published in 2001 and amended in 2005, amalgamates and revises earlier standards on access to buildings and gives detailed and thorough guidance on good practice. It is likely that this British Standard will be used as a guide to define 'reasonable provision' in relation to the Disability Discrimination Act.

This chapter looks at the relevant legislation, regulations and standards to identify the main issues affecting accessibility, disability and inclusion and to give sources of further reading and reference if required.

## The Disability Discrimination Act 1995

The Disability Discrimination Act 1995 (DDA) introduced new laws and measures to combat discrimination against disabled people. The Act gives disabled people rights in the areas of:

- recruitment and employment;
- access to goods, facilities and services;
- the management, buying or renting of land or property;
- education.

In addition, the Act allows the government to set access standards for public transport and requires schools, colleges and universities to provide information on access to education for disabled pupils and students. The Act has been amended by the Special Educational Needs and Disability Act 2001 (SENDA), which expanded the duties relating to disabled pupils and students, and by the Disability Discrimination Act 2005 (DDA 2005). The amendments are described in detail in later sections of this chapter.

The DDA is divided into a number of parts, defining disability and covering duties on different people or bodies:

- Part 1 – definition of disability;
- Part 2 – employers;
- Part 3 – providers of services, goods, facilities and those selling, letting or managing premises;
- Part 4 – education providers;
- Part 5 – transport providers.

The duties imposed by each part are similar, but not identical. Each part is considered separately in this chapter.

The Act is supplemented by regulations (secondary legislation) and statutory Codes of Practice. The DDA applies to the whole of the United Kingdom, including (as modified by Schedule 8) Northern Ireland. The Act does not apply to the Channel Islands or the Isle of Man and does not cover services or employment outside the United Kingdom.

## Codes of Practice

Each part of the DDA is supported by a Code of Practice, which explains the principles of the law, illustrates how the Act might operate in certain situations and provides general guidance on good practice. The Code of Practice does not impose legal obligations, nor is it an authoritative statement of the law; however, it can be used in evidence in legal proceedings under the Act and courts and tribunals must take account of any part of a Code of Practice that is relevant to those proceedings.

The Codes of Practice give useful explanations of considerable parts of the law, but there are some areas of ambiguity and, ultimately, it is up to the courts to decide what is lawful.

Currently it is impossible to provide definitive answers to some important questions that might be asked about parts of the law in real life situations. For example, the law does not clearly explain the basis for reasonableness and, currently, does not make clear the duties or obligations imposed on landlords to make the common parts of a building accessible for its tenants and its tenants' visitors.

The Codes of Practice are listed in Appendix B Information Sources and are available on the Disability Rights Commission website www.drc-gb.org

## Timetable for implementation

The rights granted to employees and job applicants under the DDA all came into force in December 1996. The part of the Act covering goods, facilities and services has been introduced in three stages:

- since December 1996 it has been unlawful to treat disabled people less favourably than other people for a reason related to their disability;
- since 1 October 1999 service providers have had to make reasonable adjustments for disabled people, such as providing extra help, making changes to the way a service is provided and providing auxiliary aids;
- since October 2004 there has been a duty to remove, alter or avoid physical features, or provide a reasonable alternative way of making a service available, where a physical feature makes it impossible or unreasonably difficult for disabled people to make use of services.

The implementation of duties affecting transport and education is covered later in the chapter.

## The Disability Rights Commission

The government established the Disability Rights Commission (DRC) to help eliminate discrimination against disabled people and promote equality of opportunity. The DRC also advises the government on the working of disability legislation, such as the DDA, and sponsors test cases with a view to establishing case law. The DRC writes and produces the Codes of Practice relating to the DDA.

It is likely that the DRC's functions will be integrated into the new Commission for Equality and Human Rights around the end of 2007.

## Relationship to building design

The DDA does not directly require buildings to be accessible to all disabled people and does not include standards for accessible building design; it is the services on offer within buildings that are the concern of the Act. Building designers should anticipate the needs of all building users, some of whom will fit the definition of disabled under the Act, and design accordingly. There are a great variety of ways in which employers and the providers of goods, facilities and services can comply with the requirements of the Act and only some will involve alterations to premises.

> Even if a building is designed to be accessible, this will not in itself ensure that no discrimination is taking place. Conversely, a building may be badly designed and inaccessible to people with certain physical disabilities, but the way in which the services are provided may not be seen as discriminatory under the Act.

## The meaning of discrimination

It is necessary to understand what is meant by the term discrimination as defined by the Act. In essence, discrimination occurs where a disabled person is treated less favourably than a non-disabled person for a reason relating to their disability and without justification.

> Employment opportunities and services should be provided on an equal basis, this is not necessarily the same as an identical basis. Where there are constraints due to availability of resources or the use of existing buildings, identical opportunity may be a target but equal opportunity must always be the reality.

## Actions that may be taken under the Act

A disabled person who believes that discrimination has taken place may bring civil proceedings in either an employment tribunal, for Part 2 claims, or a county court for Part 3. The DDA does not create any criminal offences. There are strict time limits for bringing actions. The time limit for a claim in an employment tribunal is 3 months and in the county court it is 6 months.

A disabled person who succeeds in an action may be awarded compensation for financial loss and injury to feelings. The court or tribunal also has the power to issue an injunction to prevent the discrimination re-occurring, and has other powers that can be used in employment disputes.

There is no limit on the size of compensation awards that can be made. There are examples of awards in excess of £20 000 being made in employment cases.

Many cases of discrimination may be unintentional and the resulting dispute may be capable of being resolved by negotiation. The Disability Rights Commission sponsors an independent conciliation service to enable disputes to be settled without the need for recourse to the courts. If this is used the time limits described above may be extended.

## DDA Part 1: definition of disability

Part 1 of the Act defines what is a disability under the Act and, therefore, who is protected under it.

It is intended that the Act should protect people who would generally be regarded as disabled. This is meant to be a fairly wide definition and extends well beyond the stereotype of a disabled person being someone using a wheelchair or a guide dog. According to the Disability Rights Commission, around one in five people of working age are considered to be disabled and likely to have rights under the DDA.

The Act defines disability as 'a physical or mental impairment which has a substantial and long-term adverse effect on a person's ability to carry out normal day-to-day activities'.

- The term 'impairment' covers physical and mental impairments; this includes sensory impairments, such as those affecting sight or hearing, and cognitive impairment, such as learning disability.

- A long-term adverse effect is one which has lasted, or is likely to last, at least 12 months or for the rest of the person's life.
- Day-to-day activities are normal activities carried out by most people on a regular basis, such as washing, eating, catching a bus or turning on a television. The person must be affected in at least one of the respects listed in the Act: mobility; manual dexterity; physical co-ordination; continence; ability to lift, carry or otherwise move everyday objects; speech, hearing or eyesight; memory or ability to concentrate, learn or understand; or perception of risk of physical danger.
- The Act also applies to some people who have had a disability in the past, for example, someone who was disabled by a mental illness but has now fully recovered.
- Any treatment or equipment that alleviates or removes the effect of an impairment is ignored when considering whether a person has a disability. The only exception to this rule is where poor eyesight is improved by wearing glasses or contact lenses. In this case the effects that count are those that remain even with the glasses or lenses.
- People with severe disfigurements are covered by the Act, without any need to demonstrate that the impairment has a substantial adverse effect on their ability to carry out normal day-to-day activities.
- Certain conditions are specifically stated not to be impairments, including addiction to or dependency on alcohol, nicotine or any other substance, hay fever and self-imposed disfigurements.

The Disability Discrimination Act 2005 amended the definition of disabled to include protection for people diagnosed with the progressive conditions of HIV, MS and cancer and removed the requirement that mental illnesses must be clinically well recognised.

**Code of Practice**    Additional information on the definition of disability is given in the Code of Practice Guidance on matters to be taken into account in determining questions relating to the definition of disability.

## DDA Part 2: employment provisions

Under the DDA, it is unlawful for employers to discriminate against disabled people in their employment or when they are applying for a job. This includes arrangements and procedures such as application forms, interview arrangements, terms of employment, promotion or training opportunities, benefits and dismissal or redundancy.

In addition, employers have a duty to make 'reasonable adjustments'. This applies where any physical feature of their premises, or any arrangements made by or on behalf of the employer, cause a substantial disadvantage to a disabled employee or job applicant. An employer has to take 'such steps as it is reasonable for him to have to take in all the circumstances' to prevent that disadvantage. Unjustified less favourable treatment and failure to make a reasonable adjustment which cannot be justified are seen by the Act as discrimination.

The employer's duty to make a reasonable adjustment comes into force when a disabled person applies for a job or an existing employee becomes disabled and requires an adjustment to be made. The duty is to an individual disabled person; it is not a general duty to disabled people at large.

All employers are covered by the employment provision of the Act with the exception of the Armed Forces.

### Adjustments that an employer might have to make

Examples given in the Act of adjustments that an employer might have to make are:

- making adjustments to premises;
- reallocating part of a job to another employee;
- transferring the disabled person to fill an existing vacancy;
- altering the person's working hours;
- assigning the person to a different place of work;
- allowing absences during working hours for rehabilitation, assessment or treatment;
- supplying additional training;
- acquiring special equipment or modifying existing equipment;
- modifying instructions or reference manuals;

- modifying procedures for testing or assessment;
- providing a reader or interpreter;
- providing additional supervision.

---

When staff undergo appraisals or reviews as part of their employment it is important that everyone is given an equal opportunity to perform to the best of his or her ability, especially if promotion or pay increases depend upon the outcome.

If the appraisal process, or perhaps the room in which the interview takes place, does not allow someone who has a disability to perform as well as non-disabled people, it is likely that he or she is being discriminated against.

Facilities such as inductions loops, appropriate seating, adequate lighting, good acoustics and, if necessary, interpreters should be provided where needed to ensure everyone has the opportunity to maximise his or her performance in such important assessments.

After all – isn't that usually the purpose of the exercise?

---

The Act lists a number of factors which may have a bearing on whether it will be reasonable for the employer to have to make a particular adjustment. The factors are:

- the effectiveness of the particular adjustment in preventing the disadvantage;
- the practicability of the adjustment;
- the financial and other costs of the adjustment and the extent of any disruption caused;
- the extent of the employer's financial or other resources;
- the availability to the employer of financial or other assistance to help make an adjustment.

In practice, most adjustments will not involve alterations to physical features, often involve little or no cost or disruption and are therfore very likely to be considered reasonable.

**Trade organisations and qualifications bodies**  The Act makes it unlawful for a trade organisation to discriminate against a disabled person in relation to membership of the organisation or access to membership benefits. The Act also makes it unlawful for a qualifications body to discriminate against a disabled person in relation to conferring professional or trade qualifications.

The Act says that it is unlawful for a trade organisation to discriminate against a disabled person:

- in the arrangements it makes for the purpose of determining who should be offered membership of the organisation; or
- in the terms on which it is prepared to admit him to membership; or
- by refusing to accept, or deliberately not accepting, his application for membership.

The Act also says that it is unlawful for a trade organisation to discriminate against a disabled member:

- in the way it affords the member access to any benefits or by refusing or deliberately omitting to afford access to them; or
- by depriving the member of membership, or varying the terms of his membership; or
- by subjecting the member to any other detriment.

In relation to conferring professional or trade qualifications, the Act says that it is unlawful for a qualifications body to discriminate against a disabled person:

- in the arrangements it makes for the purpose of determining upon whom to confer a professional or trade qualification, or
- in the terms on which it is prepared to confer such a qualification, or
- by refusing or deliberately omitting to grant any application by him for a professional or trade qualification, or
- by withdrawing such a qualification from him or varying the terms on which he holds it.

In addition to what it says about discrimination, Part 2 makes it unlawful for either a trade organisation or a qualifications body to subject a disabled person to harassment for a reason which relates to his disability. It is also unlawful for a person who has authority or influence over another to instruct him, or put pressure on him, to act unlawfully under the provisions of Part 2. This covers pressure to discriminate, whether applied directly to the person concerned, or indirectly but in a way in which he is likely to hear of it. However, the Act does not give individual disabled people the right to take legal action in respect of unlawful instructions or pressure to discriminate. Such action may only be taken by the DRC.

The Act also covers advertisements for membership of trade organisations or for professional or trade qualifications.

> If a trade organisation offers members services such as conference or training opportunities, they must be offered in a way that is accessible to all members who wish to attend. This would include the venue where the event is held, any accompanying notes, presentations and all other parts of the service.

**Codes of Practice**    There are two Codes of Practice giving guidance on the operation of Part 2 of the Act: Code of Practice Employment and Occupation and Code of Practice Trade Organisations and Qualifications Bodies. Both are available on the DRC website.

> There is no minimum standard of adjustments to premises required by the DDA, but the employment Code of Practice gives examples of possible adjustments that it might be reasonable for an employer to make. These include: widening a doorway, providing a ramp or moving furniture for a wheelchair user; relocating light switches, door handles or shelves for someone who has difficulty in reaching; and providing appropriate contrast in décor.

## DDA Part 3: access to goods, facilities and services

Part 3 of the DDA deals with access to goods, facilities, services and premises. It is based on the principle that disabled people should not be treated less favourably simply because of their disability, by those who provide goods, facilities and services to the public.

Throughout this section reference is made to 'service providers' for convenience. Subject to certain exceptions, Part 3 of the DDA applies to any person or any organisation or entity that is concerned with the provision of services, including the provision of goods and facilities, to the public or a section of the public. It is irrelevant whether a service is provided on payment or without payment.

Part 3 of the Disability Discrimination Act 1995 has been amended by the Disability Discrimination Act 2005. The changes affect:

- public authorities, some of whose functions had previously not been covered by the Act;
- private clubs whose activities regarding their members had previously not been covered by the Act;
- the housing sector, with new duties being placed on those letting, controlling and managing property.

There are no changes to the duties of those already covered by Part 3 of the DDA (for example service providers such as shops and restaurants).

The new duties are described in detail in the section of this chapter covering the Disability Discrimination Act 2005.

**Services covered**   The Code of Practice relating to Part 3 of the Act gives a list of some of the services that are covered. These include local councils, government departments and agencies, the emergency services, charities, voluntary organisations, hotels, restaurants, pubs, post offices, banks, building societies, solicitors, accountants, telecommunications and broadcasting organisations, public utilities, national parks, sports stadia, leisure centres, advice agencies, theatres, cinemas, hairdressers, shops, market stalls, petrol stations, telesales businesses, places of worship, courts, hospitals and clinics.

**Figure 3.1** A low ticket desk can help a service provider fulfil their duties under the DDA.

The Act says that services include 'access to and use of any place which members of the public are permitted to enter'. Thus a person who permits members of the public to enter such a place is providing a service to those people consisting of access to and use of that place.

Amendments made to the DDA as a result of the 2005 Act mean that, for example, it will be unlawful not to provide equal service to disabled people in a train buffet car.

Transport providers have duties under Part 3 of the Act, relating to infrastructure, information and services, to avoid discrimination and make reasonable adjustments to, for example, timetables, booking facilities, waiting rooms and other facilities at ferry terminals or bus, coach or rail stations. Part 3 of the 1995 Act does not cover vehicles; however, the Disability Discrimination Act 2005 extends the law to the use of certain transport vehicles. This will mean that disabled people can expect equal service when boarding, travelling and disembarking from public transport vehicles.

Further information is given on transport, and the changes to the law made by the DDA 2005, in the section of this chapter covering Part 5 of the Act.

Education was excluded from Part 3 of the Act up until September 2002, when the Special Educational Needs and Disability Act 2001 removed the exemption. Further information is given on education in the section of this chapter looking at Part 4 of the Act.

Part 3 of the Act does not cover manufacture and design of products, as this does not involve the provision of services direct to the public.

**Part 3 duties**   The duties under this part of the Act were introduced in three stages. The first rights of access came into effect from December 1996. Since then there has been a duty on service providers not to discriminate against disabled people by:

- refusing to provide, or deliberately not providing, a service which is offered to other people;
- offering a lower standard or worse manner of service; or
- offering less favourable terms.

From October 1999, service providers have been required to make reasonable adjustments to allow disabled people to use a service. This duty applies when access to a service is impossible or unreasonably difficult. The duty was introduced in two stages. The first stage, which took effect from October 1999, requires service providers to take reasonable steps to:

- make reasonable adjustments to policies, procedures or practices which exclude disabled people or make it unreasonably difficult for disabled people to use the service – an example would be exempting working dogs from a 'no dogs' policy in a restaurant;

- provide auxiliary aids or services, such as the provision of information on audio cassette, which would enable disabled people to use a service; and
- where a physical feature is a barrier to service, finding a reasonable alternative method of delivering the service.

The duties that came into force from October 1999 did not require service providers to do anything that would necessitate making a permanent alteration to the physical fabric of their premises. The duties affected the way in which buildings are used and managed. Duties relating to alterations to physical features came into force in 2004.

From October 2004, service providers have had a duty to take such steps 'as are reasonable in all the circumstances of the case' to modify physical features of premises which make it impossible or unreasonably difficult for disabled people to use the service or to provide the service by a reasonable alternative method. There are four different options which are available to a service provider to comply with this duty. In essence these are to:

- remove the feature;
- alter the feature so it no longer has the effect of making it impossible or unreasonably difficult for disabled people to use the service;
- provide a reasonable means of avoiding the feature; or
- provide a reasonable alternative method of making the service available to disabled people.

**Reasonableness in service provision**   Section 21 of the Act refers to a service provider being under a duty to take such steps as it is reasonable, in all the circumstances of the case, for it to have to take in order to make reasonable adjustments. What is a reasonable step will vary according to:

- the type of services being provided;
- the nature of the service provider and its size and resources;
- the effect of the disability on the individual disabled person.

It is not possible to assess reasonableness just in terms of cost, as this is only one issue to be taken into account. The Code of Practice relating to Part 3 of the Act gives a list of factors, which might be taken into account when considering what is reasonable:

- whether taking any particular steps would be effective in overcoming the difficulty that disabled people face in accessing the service in question;
- the extent to which it is practicable for the service provider to take the steps;
- the financial and other costs of making the adjustment;
- the extent of any disruption which taking the steps would cause;
- the extent of the service provider's financial and other resources;
- the amount of any resources already spent on making adjustments;
- the availability of financial or other assistance.

There is no exemption for small service providers, though it is likely that what is seen as a reasonable step for a large retailer with multiple outlets to take will not necessarily be seen as reasonable for a corner shop.

> It is important to realise that there is no 'one size fits all' solution to meeting obligations under the DDA, for service providers or employers. Even an identical barrier to access in two identical buildings may well need to be addressed in different ways, according to the several issues described above.
>
> What is necessary is to consider each situation on its merits and not try to simply apply general solutions.

The Code of Practice contains examples of how the duties on service providers are intended to operate, and how the concept of reasonableness is to be interpreted in relation to the duty to make adjustments and provide auxiliary aids. It is clear that the duty is a continuing one, and is owed disabled people at large. It is described as 'an evolving duty, not something that simply needs to be considered once and once only, and then forgotten. What was originally a reasonable step to take might no longer be sufficient and the provision of further or different adjustments might then have to be considered'.

> Service providers should plan ahead to anticipate the requirements of disabled people and the adjustments that may have to be made for them. They should not wait until a disabled person wants to use the service.

The Code of Practice also notes that service providers should bear in mind that there are no hard and fast solutions. 'Actions which may result in reasonable access to services being achieved for some disabled people may not necessarily do so for others. Equally, it is not enough for service providers to make some changes if they still leave their services impossible or unreasonably difficult for disabled people to use.'

> The DDA expressly states that a service provider is not required to take any step 'which would fundamentally alter the nature of the service in question or his trade, profession or business'. Therefore, if a factor is inherent to the nature of the service being provided, such as low lighting in a nightclub, the service provider is not required to alter the service to make it fully accessible to disabled people. However, a decision of this sort would have to be defended if challenged.

**Auxiliary aids and services**   An auxiliary aid or service might be the provision of a special piece of equipment or simply extra assistance to disabled people from staff. The Code of Practice gives examples of auxiliary aids and services including the provision of information on audiotape and the provision of a sign language interpreter.

## Reasonable steps in relation to auxiliary aids and services

The Code of Practice gives guidance on the range of auxiliary aids and services which it might be reasonable to provide to ensure that services are accessible to people with hearing disabilities:

- written information, such as a leaflet or a guide;
- a facility for taking and exchanging written notes;
- a verbatim speech-to-text transcription service;
- non-permanent induction loop systems;
- subtitles;
- videos with sign language interpretation;
- information displayed on a computer screen;
- accessible websites;
- textphones, telephone amplifiers and inductive couplers;
- teletext displays;
- audio-visual telephones;
- audio-visual fire alarms (not involving physical alterations to premises);
- qualified sign language interpreters or lipspeakers.

For people with visual impairments, the range of auxiliary aids and services which it might be reasonable to provide include the following:

- readers;
- documents in large or clear print, Moon or Braille;
- information on computer disk;
- information on audio tape;
- telephone services to supplement other information;
- spoken announcements or verbal communication;
- accessible websites;
- assistance with guiding;
- audio description services;
- large print or tactile maps, plans and three-dimensional models;
- touch facilities.

Auxiliary aids and services are not limited to aids to communication. A portable temporary ramp will also fall into this category, as will other items that assist physical access but do not involve a permanent alteration to the physical features or fabric of the building.

## Physical features   A physical feature includes:

- any feature arising from the design or construction of a building on the premises occupied by the service provider;
- any feature on those premises or any approach to, exit from or access to such a building;
- any fixtures, fittings, furnishings, furniture, equipment or materials in or on such premises.

All such features are covered whether temporary or permanent.

## Duties relating to physical features   The Act states that where there is a physical feature that makes it impossible or unreasonably difficult for a disabled person to make use of a

**Figure 3.2**  A platform lift can be used to overcome a physical feature such as a stepped change of level.

service, service providers have to take reasonable steps to remove, alter or avoid it (for example, by installing a permanent ramp to enable wheelchair users to gain access to premises previously reached only by steps) if the service cannot be provided by a reasonable alternative method. The Act does not give any guidance on which of these approaches the service provider should take.

The Code of Practice, however, does state that service providers should adopt an 'inclusive' approach and consider first whether a physical feature which creates a barrier for disabled people can be removed or altered. The reasons given for recommending this approach are:

- the service will be available to everyone in the same way;
- it is preferable to any alternative arrangements from the standpoint of the dignity of disabled people;
- it is likely to be in the long-term interests of the service provider, since it will avoid the ongoing costs of providing the service by alternative means and may expand the customer base.

The Code of Practice recommends that only when removal or alteration is not reasonable should the service provider consider providing a means of avoiding the feature. If that is also not reasonable, the service provider should then consider providing a reasonable alternative method of making the service available to disabled people.

The law does not require a service provider to adopt one way of meeting its obligations rather than another. The Act is concerned with the end result and that the service is accessible to disabled people, rather than how this is achieved. However, if a service remains inaccessible, a service provider may have to defend its decision to adopt a certain approach.

If a service provider decides to use the option of providing a service by an alternative method and disabled people are then able to access that service without unreasonable difficulty, the obligations of the service provider under the Act will be satisfied. However, if it is still unreasonably difficult for the disabled person to use the service, the service provider would then have to show that it could not have reasonably removed or altered the physical feature, or provided a reasonable means of avoiding it. The cost of removing, altering or avoiding might be a relevant consideration. If a service provider takes no action it will have to show that there were no steps that it could reasonably have taken.

There are circumstances in which the duty to make reasonable adjustments is affected by compliance with the Building Regulations. More detail is given on this subject in the section on Building Regulations and the DDA.

**Reasonable adjustments in practice**    Physical alterations will not always be the most appropriate way to improve the access to a service. Often measures such as disability awareness training for staff or simply allowing more time to serve disabled customers will be all that is required to make a service accessible. However, there will be situations when adjustments in the form of physical alterations are necessary.

The Code of Practice suggests that:

'regularly reviewing the way in which it provides its services to the public, for example via periodic disability audits, might help a service provider identify any less obvious or unintentional barriers to access for disabled people. Obtaining the views of disabled customers and disabled employees will also assist a service provider. Disabled people know best what hurdles they face in trying to use the services provided. They can identify difficulties in accessing services and might also suggest solutions involving the provision of reasonable adjustments.'

**The role of access audits**    The Code of Practice clearly suggests that service providers are more likely to be able to comply with their duty to make adjustments in relation to physical features if they arrange for an access audit of their premises to be conducted and draw up an access plan or strategy. It states that 'acting on the results of such an evaluation may reduce the likelihood of legal claims against the service provider'. However, undertaking an access audit is not a specific requirement of the DDA.

There may be situations where it is not reasonable for a service provider to anticipate a particular requirement. However, where a disabled person has pointed out the difficulty that he or she faces in accessing services, or has suggested a reasonable solution to that difficulty, it might then become reasonable for the service provider to take a particular step to meet these requirements.

**A continuing and evolving duty**   The duty to make reasonable adjustments is a continuing duty that should be regularly reviewed. The Code of Practice describes it as:

'an evolving duty, not something that simply needs to be considered once and once only, and then forgotten. What was originally a reasonable step to take might no longer be sufficient and the provision of further or different adjustments might then have to be considered.'

Technological developments may provide new or improved solutions to certain problems and what was once an unreasonable step might become reasonable.

Examples range from the use of personal items such as mobile phones to the use of Global Information Systems (GIS) by, for example, transport providers. The possibilities for technological developments are boundless – and costs are becoming more affordable.

**Justification of less favourable treatment or failure to make reasonable adjustments**   In limited circumstances, the Act does permit a service provider to justify the less favourable treatment of a disabled person or a failure to make a reasonable adjustment. The justifications include: health and safety

**Figure 3.3** Seating should be provided in waiting areas. Armrests are helpful for some people.

considerations; incapacity to enter into a contract; the service provider being otherwise unable to provide the service to the public; enabling the service provider to provide the service to the disabled person or other members of the public; and the greater cost of providing a tailor-made service.

> For a justification of discrimination to apply, the court must be satisfied that the service provider believed that one or more of the specified conditions existed and that it was reasonable for him or her to hold that opinion.

**Health and safety**   The Act does not require a service provider to do anything that would endanger the health and safety of any person, including the disabled person in question. However, health and safety reasons that rely on prejudice or stereotyping of disabled people are no defence.

A cinema might not be justified in refusing entry to a wheelchair user based on an assumption that they would be a hazard in a fire. It is the responsibility of the management to make any special provision needed.

The Code of Practice explains that service providers should ensure that any action taken in relation to health and safety is proportionate to the risk. There must be a balance between protecting against the risk and restricting disabled people from using the service. Disabled people are entitled to take the same risks within the same limits as other people.

Before using health and safety to justify less favourable treatment, a service provider should consider whether a reasonable adjustment could be made to allow the disabled person to access the service safely.

**Incapacity to contract**    The Act does not require a service provider to contract with a disabled person who is incapable of entering into a legally enforceable contract or of giving an informed consent. However, the service provider should assume that a disabled person is able to enter into any contract and if there is a problem consider whether a reasonable adjustment could be made to solve it.

An example of a reasonable adjustment might be to prepare a contract document in plain English to aid understanding.

**Service provider otherwise unable to provide the service to the public**    A service provider can justify refusing to provide a service to a disabled person if this is necessary because the service provider would otherwise be unable to provide the service to other members of the public. However, this justification will only hold if other people would be effectively prevented from using the service. It is not enough that those other people would be simply inconvenienced or delayed.

An example given in the Code of Practice is if a tour guide refuses to allow a person with severe mobility impairment on a tour of old city walls because he or she has well-founded reasons to believe that the extra help the guide would have to give him or her would prevent the party from completing the tour. This is likely to be justified.

**To enable the service provider to provide the service to the disabled person or other members of the public**   A service provider can justify providing service of a lower standard or in a worse manner or on worse terms if this is necessary in order to be able to provide the service to the disabled person or other members of the public.

Again, before a service provider uses this condition as a justification it should consider whether a reasonable adjustment could be made to allow the disabled person access to the service.

**Greater cost of providing a tailor-made service**   If a service is individually tailored to the needs of a disabled person, the service provider can justify charging more for this service. However, justification on this ground cannot apply where the extra cost results from the provision of a reasonable adjustment.

**Property owners and managers**   The Act introduces particular duties on landlords and others who sell, let or manage premises. It is unlawful for a person with power to dispose of any premises to discriminate against a disabled person:

- in the terms of disposal of the premises;
- by refusing to dispose of the premises to the disabled person;
- in the treatment of the disabled person.

Disposing of the premises includes selling, letting, or assigning a tenancy. It does not include the hire of premises or booking of rooms in a hotel, as these would be covered by provisions relating to services.

In addition, those managing premises have a duty not to discriminate against a disabled person occupying the premises:

- in the way he/she permits the disabled person to make use of any benefits or facilities;
- by refusing to permit use of those facilities or by deliberately omitting permission;
- by evicting the disabled person or subjecting them to any other detriment.

It is also unlawful for a person whose licence or consent is required for the disposal of any leased or sub-let premises to discriminate against a disabled person by withholding that licence or consent.

As elsewhere in the Act, discrimination occurs when a disabled person is treated less favourably for a reason relating to his or her disability and when that treatment cannot be justified.

> There is no duty to make reasonable adjustments to premises that are sold, let or managed. However, improving the accessibility of building stock may well increase potential value and ease of letting.

**Exemptions in disposal of premises**    The provisions described above do not apply to owner-occupiers if:

- that person owns an estate or interest in the premises; and
- wholly occupies the premises.

However, if the owner-occupier uses the services of an estate agent or publishes an advertisement for the purpose of disposing of the premises, the Act applies.

**Small dwellings exemption**    The provisions of the Act prohibiting discrimination against disabled people in the disposal of premises do not apply to certain 'small dwellings' (houses or other residential property). The Act gives a number of conditions that must be satisfied for the exemption to apply:

- the relevant occupier must live on the premises, intend to continue doing so and be sharing accommodation on the premises with other people who are not members of their household, for example, a multi-occupancy residential building with shared accommodation;
- the shared accommodation must not be storage accommodation or means of access;
- the premises must be 'small premises' as defined by the Act.

### Justification of less favourable treatment in relation to premises

Less favourable treatment of a disabled person for a reason relating to disability amounts to discrimination unless that treatment can be shown to be justified. The Act sets out conditions that could apply to justify such treatment. These conditions are similar to the conditions that apply to justifying discrimination in the provision of services and the general approach to justification is the same.

### Changes to the law from 2006

From December 2006, the DDA 2005 extends duties on landlords and managers of premises to include a duty to make reasonable adjustments to policies, practices and procedures, and to provide auxiliary aids and services, to enable a disabled person to rent a property and to facilitate a disabled tenant's enjoyment of the premises. There is no duty to make physical adjustments either to the premises themselves, or to any common parts of the building in which the premises are located. However, there is provision for residential tenants whose landlords refuse to consent to their making improvements that are intended to facilitate their enjoyment of the property. Where a landlord unreasonably withholds consent in these circumstances, consent is deemed to have been given.

> When the law is extended in December 2006, a landlord or manager may be obliged to allow a tenant who has mobility difficulties to leave her rubbish in another place if she cannot access the designated place.

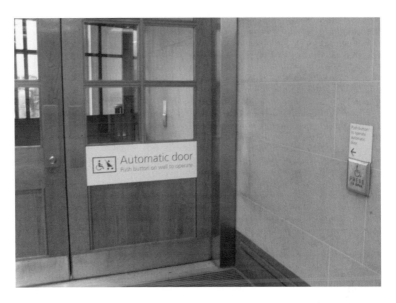

**Figure 3.4** Adding automatic opening to doors can make access more convenient and help a service provider fulfil their duties under the DDA.

The DDA 2005 also confers a power to modify or end the small dwelling exemption from December 2006.

Further information on rental and management of premises is given in the section covering the 2005 Act in this chapter.

**Other issues covered by Part 3 of the DDA**  The Act and the associated regulations affect the provision of particular services, such as insurance, guarantees and deposits. These issues are covered in the Code of Practice relating to Part 3.

## Obtaining necessary consents

Nothing in the DDA removes the need for any necessary consent to be obtained where this is required under general law or under a contract or lease, but in some cases regulations set out what sort of action is reasonable in terms of seeking such consent.

Consents may also be needed from mortgagees or neighbours, for example, an adjoining owner with the benefit of a restrictive covenant preventing alterations being made. In these cases the employer or service provider must seek consent but need not make any alteration until that consent has been obtained.

There are extensive provisions relating to the obtaining of land-lord's consent. The Codes of Practice set out the procedures in considerable detail.

## Statutory consents

A service provider may have to obtain statutory consents such as planning permission, building regulation approval, listed building consent or fire regulations approval, before carrying out alterations to physical features. The Act does not override the need to obtain such consents. Where consent is refused, there is likely to be a means of appeal. Whether the service provider has a duty to appeal will depend on the circumstances of the case.

> Applying for consent is always a reasonable step to take, but the employer or service provider might have to consider whether it is reasonable to make a temporary adjustment in the meantime, or adopt a different permanent adjustment not requiring consent.

## Building Regulations and the DDA

The duty under Part 3 of the DDA to make reasonable adjust-ments to physical features of buildings can be affected by building regulation compliance. Where the physical features of a building met the requirements of Part M of the Building Regulations (or its equivalent in Northern Ireland or Scotland) at the time of its construction, and continue to meet them, a service provider may not have to make any further adjustment to those features. Even if the exemption applies so that no physical adjustment is required, there may still be an obligation to make an alternative adjustment if a reasonable one can be identified, or to provide the service in another manner.

This exemption does not apply to employers under Part 2 of the Act. The exemption under Part 3 is only available for a period of 10 years from the date when a feature was constructed.

Further information is given in the section on Building Regulations in this chapter.

## DDA Part 4: education

Part 4 of the DDA requires education institutions in England and Wales to inform parents, pupils and students about their arrangements for disabled people. From January 1997 the governing bodies of all maintained schools, except special schools, have had to publish in their annual reports:

- a description of the admission arrangements for disabled pupils;
- details of the steps taken to prevent disabled pupils from being treated less favourably;
- details of facilities provided to assist access to the school for disabled pupils.

The Act also places new duties on Further Education Funding Councils and Higher Education Funding Councils.

Part 3 of the DDA initially excluded publicly funded education from the provisions relating to goods, facilities and services. The exemption of education was effectively removed by the Special Educational Needs and Disability Act 2001, which came into force in September 2002.

**Special Educational Needs and Disability Act 2001**   The Special Educational Needs and Disability Act 2001 (SENDA) amended Part 4 of the DDA and expanded the duties relating to disabled pupils and students. It also removed the exemption of publicly funded education from Part 3 of the Act, though where a Part 4 duty applies, Part 3 cannot apply. Education providers are now required to make 'reasonable adjustments' for disabled students and pupils. These new duties cover all areas of education, schools, colleges, universities, adult education and youth services, and include:

- a duty not to treat disabled students/pupils less favourably than non-disabled students/pupils without justification;

**Figure 3.5**  Access is not just a matter of ramps and WCs – playgrounds should be accessible too.

- a duty to make reasonable adjustments to policies, procedures and practices that may discriminate against disabled students/pupils;
- a duty to provide education by a 'reasonable alternative means' where a physical feature places a disabled student/pupil at a substantial disadvantage (there is no general duty to remove or alter physical features or provide auxiliary aids or services);
- a duty on local education authorities in England and Wales to plan strategically and increase the overall accessibility to school premises and the curriculum.

Post-16 education providers have further duties, which come into force as follows:

- from September 2002 they have had a duty not to discriminate against existing and prospective disabled students by treating them less favourably than others in the provision of student services;
- from September 2003 they have had a duty to make reasonable adjustments and provide auxiliary aids;

- from September 2005 there has been a duty to make reasonable adjustments to physical features.

The duty to make adjustments to physical features is an anticipatory and continuing duty. Further and higher education providers are required to consider the needs of disabled people in general and not wait until an existing or prospective student requires a reasonable adjustment to be made.

The Disability Discrimination Act 2005 places a new duty on all public sector authorities, including education providers, to promote disability equality. This duty is described in more detail in the section of this chapter covering the DDA 2005.

## DDA Part 5: transport

Part 5 of the DDA deals with public transport vehicles. It allows the government to set accessibility standards for buses, coaches, trains, trams and taxis. The regulations set minimum technical requirements to ensure that disabled people can use public transport safely and comfortably. Areas covered include size of door openings, dimensions of seating compartments, visual contrast, ramps on platforms to allow access to trains and accessible WC facilities on trains.

Transport infrastructure is covered by Part 3 of the Act. The sorts of activities covered by this are likely to include:

- the sale of tickets (including ticket machines);
- transport information in all forms (including timetables, station announcement systems and screens, information phone lines and websites);
- the physical environment of stations from entrance to the platform or bus stop;
- the services of transport staff at the station or at a travel information centre.

The Disability Discrimination Act 2005, and regulations made under it, make a number of changes to the Disability Discrimination Act 1995 (DDA). In particular, the law is extended to the use of certain transport vehicles.

The change to the law will mean that from the end of 2006 the DDA will cover the use of the vehicle itself. This will include getting on and off and the service received while travelling on the vehicle.

These duties will apply to buses and coaches, taxis and private hire vehicles, trains, trams and light railways, rental cars and breakdown recovery vehicles.

At present there are no plans to include planes and ferries within the new duties, although the power to do so at a later date is included in the DDA 2005. However, the service infrastructure, such as airports and ferry ports, is already covered by existing Part 3 duties.

The DDA, as amended, says that people providing transport services must make reasonable adjustments to their services so that they are accessible to disabled people. This duty is anticipatory and transport providers should expect that disabled people will be getting on, travelling on and getting off their vehicles. They should consider what adjustments might be needed and put the necessary arrangements in place without waiting to be asked.

Transport providers will be required to take reasonable steps to change a policy, practice or procedure which makes it impossible or very difficult for a disabled person to get on or off a vehicle, or to use any services on the vehicle, such as a buffet car. They will also be required to take reasonable steps to provide an auxiliary aid or service, broadly, any kind of extra help, to a disabled person so that they can get on, travel on and get off a vehicle or use any services on the vehicle.

In addition, providers of rental cars and breakdown services may be expected to make changes relating to physical barriers preventing disabled people from using their vehicles.

Companies providing rental vehicles will have to take reasonable steps to remove, alter or avoid a physical feature which prevents a disabled person using a vehicle, or find a reasonable and different way of offering their service. Breakdown recovery companies will have to overcome physical features that present barriers to disabled people by providing the service in a reasonable alternative way.

The Disability Rights Commission has written a supplement to the Part 3 Code of Practice covering provision and use of transport vehicles.

# The Disability Discrimination Act 2005

The Disability Discrimination Act 2005 (DDA 2005) extends the scope, range, application and duties imposed by the DDA 1995. The 2005 Act does not replace the 1995 Act; it addresses a number of issues that were either omitted from the DDA 1995, or which had proved to be insufficient, unenforceable, or had not been brought fully into effect. It does this by amending the provisions of and inserting new sections into the 1995 Act.

The 2005 Act extends civil rights in areas of the provision of transport services, letting of premises, the responsibilities and duties of public authorities, membership of private clubs, and the rights of disabled councillors. It also broadens the definition of disability contained in the DDA 1995.

## Public authorities

The 2005 Act extends the DDA to prohibit discrimination in relation to every function of a public authority. Public authorities include, for example, local authorities, government departments and NHS trusts and boards. However, the specific provisions relating to public functions will only apply where other parts of the Act do not already apply. For example, where a public authority is providing a service to the public or employing or educating someone, the provisions of the Act relating to service to the public, employment or education will apply. The duties imposed on public authorities when providing a service and those imposed when carrying out a function are broadly similar.

There are some public authorities which are excluded from these provisions. These are:

- both Houses of Parliament;
- a person exercising functions in connection with proceedings in Parliament;
- the Security Service and Secret Intelligence Service; and
- the Government Communications Headquarters including any part of the Armed Forces assisting it in carrying out its functions.

**What is a public function?**  In its broadest sense, public functions can be regarded as all the activities of a public body. Some of these will be covered by the 1995 Act; for example, Part 3 of the DDA 1995 already places a duty on public bodies, such as the police and local authorities, not to discriminate in the way they provide their services. This might include access to information and guidance on crime prevention, providing general guidance on how to access benefits and other assistance, and access to public facilities.

> In arresting and detaining someone, it is thought that the police, who are the only body with the authority to do so, are not offering a service to the public but are exercising a public function.

Examples of activities covered by the 2005 Act are as follows:

- procedures such as consultation in planning applications and in the preparation of local plans;
- the functions of the probation service and prison service in terms of, for example, the preparation of pre-sentencing reports and the revoking of community sentences, prison discipline and prison escort services;
- the granting of licences by public bodies for activities such as charitable collections, public entertainment and performances, street trading;
- the publishing of documents such as annual reports and statutory plans.

The nature of the duty placed on public authorities by the 2005 Act closely follows the anticipatory duty placed on service providers by Part 3 of the DDA 1995.

## The public sector duty to promote equality of opportunity for disabled people

Under the DDA 1995, there is no duty for public authorities to ensure that their activities encourage equal opportunities and improve opportunities for disabled people. The 2005 Act addressed this shortfall by introducing a positive statutory duty on public authorities to promote equality of opportunity for disabled people in all the public functions they undertake. To do this, it creates a Public Sector Duty on Discrimination, which has two parts. The first is a general duty to eliminate unlawful discrimination against disabled people, and the second is a duty to promote and monitor equality of opportunity.

**The general duty**    The 2005 Act provides that bodies undertaking public functions must take account of disability equality in their everyday work, which includes, for example, policy making, the delivery of services, employment practices and the functions they undertake in their role as a public body.

The general duty on a public body requires each authority to identify the areas that are likely to have the greatest impact on improving opportunities for disabled people, and act on them.

Clearly, within the public sector, the relevance of particular policies and the importance placed on them will vary from authority to authority. For example, the maintenance of a pedestrian streetscape or communication policies may be more relevant for some than, for example, the management of waste disposal. However, in reality it would be difficult to imagine any functions within the public sector that are not highly relevant to disabled people.

**Specific duties**    The 2005 Act also introduces specific duties to promote a cycle of performance improvement that will help public bodies to progress towards the goal of greater equality for disabled people. To assist public authorities to carry out the general duty not to discriminate and to promote equality, specific duties in relation to employment and service delivery will be imposed on some authorities. These authorities include local authorities, government departments, colleges and schools and other bodies with a public role such as the Audit Commission and the Housing Corporation.

**A disability equality scheme**   One specific duty is for the relevant public bodies to develop a Disability Equality Scheme (DES). The DES must set out how the public body fulfils its duties to eliminate unlawful discrimination and the harassment of disabled people, and how it will promote the equality of opportunity. They will also be required to produce an action plan to identify how and when the DES will be monitored, reviewed and updated. It is recommended that the DES will be the subject of an annual progress review, and revision within three years of its publication.

**Reasonable adjustments**   Public bodies are expected to undertake adjustments to the physical environment or to their practices, policies and procedures that are reasonable in all the circumstances of the case.

> As many of the functions of public bodies are also carried out in buildings from which they also deliver services already covered by the DDA 1995, and for which accessibility should have been fully addressed since October 2004, it is not expected that many physical adjustments to premises will be needed to meet the duties imposed by the 2005 Act. However, that is unlikely to be the case in terms of the practices, policies and procedures currently adopted.

**Justification for discrimination**   As with the duties placed on service providers and employers by the DDA 1995, the 2005 Act allows for public sector bodies to provide less favourable treatment, or, in some circumstances, fail to make a reasonable adjustment, if it can be justified. In such cases, justification may be claimed if, for example:

- there are substantiated health and safety reasons;
- the cost of undertaking any alterations is unreasonable given all the circumstances of the particular case;
- complying with the duties imposed on the body adversely affects the rights of others;

- the authority believes that the disabled person is incapable of entering into an enforceable agreement, or of giving informed consent.

## Private clubs

The 2005 Act places a duty on private clubs with 25 or more members not to discriminate against disabled people, including members, bringing them into line with the duties already imposed by the DDA 1995 on service providers such as shops, restaurants and theatres.

The 2005 Act covers larger organisations with a controlled membership, such as a private social or sports club, some professional societies, and political parties, which it defines as 'any association of 25 or more persons, whether incorporated or unincorporated, and whether run for profit or not'.

An association for this purpose must operate a genuine policy of membership selection based on personal criteria so as to distinguish between members of the association and members of the public. A club that does not operate such a policy of membership selection is already covered by the Part 3 duties imposed by the DDA 1995 where it provides services to the public or a section of the public.

Unless it has a justification for doing so, the 2005 Act provides that an anticipatory duty is placed on the club to make reasonable adjustments and, as currently applicable to Part 3 of the DDA 1995:

- not to discriminate against a disabled person. This will involve treating a disabled person less favourably for a reason relating to their disability compared to a person who is not disabled, without justification;
- to make reasonable adjustments to policies, practices and procedures and also to physical features;
- to make available auxiliary aids and services.

This gives new rights to disabled people who are:

- applicants for membership of the private club;
- existing members of the club;

- associates (people who as members of a private club have the right to enter other clubs);
- guests invited by the club or its members;
- people eligible to be guests of the club.

## Definition of disability

The 2005 Act extends the definition of disability stated in the 1995 Act to cover people with progressive conditions such as, for example, multiple sclerosis, HIV infection and cancer from diagnosis, rather than, as under the 1995 Act, from the point at which their impairment has an adverse effect on their ability to carry out normal day-to-day activities.

> The extension of the definition of disability will afford the protection of the DDA to the period between the diagnosis of a condition and an effect being apparent, a time when disabled people have been liable to experience discrimination.

The 2005 Act also removes the requirement in the 1995 Act for a mental illness to be clinically well diagnosed before it can be considered as a mental impairment. However, a person with a mental illness will still have to show that their impairment has a long-term and substantial adverse effect on their ability to carry out normal day-to-day activities.

## Rental and management of premises

**Duties on landlords and managers**   The DDA 2005 introduces a duty to make adjustments in relation to premises provision. However, there is still no duty on landlords to remove or make changes to physical features that make a property difficult to access. The landlord may also be able to justify a failure to make a reasonable adjustment if it can be shown that, in the particular circumstance, such changes would have been unreasonable. These circumstances could relate to proven health and safety issues or if the disabled person was incapable of entering into an enforceable agreement, or of giving informed consent.

Examples of changes that could be made to assist the letting process include, for example, providing paperwork in alternative formats, assessing the way the property is managed, and changing, if reasonable to do so, any terms in the letting which might prevent a disabled person renting or using the property.

This latter action might include, for example:

- not unreasonably withholding consent for the tenant to carry out minor alterations to their own building, or to install a stair lift within their own building, if they wish to do so at their own cost of installation and reinstatement;
- waiving the terms of letting to allow a tenant to keep an assistance dog on the premises;
- allowing a tenant with limited mobility to leave their rubbish in another place if they cannot access the designated area.

A landlord or manager will also have to take reasonable steps to provide an auxiliary aid or service if it would assist a disabled tenant enjoying the premises or any associated benefit or facility. Examples here could include:

- using larger font in correspondence letters and details to assist someone who is visually impaired;
- supplying a simple adaptation to a door bell facility to assist someone who is deaf or hard of hearing;
- providing a temporary ramp to overcome a step into or within the property.

However, the duty for the landlord or manager to provide an auxiliary aid or service will only arise if it is specifically needed for the use of the premises. A landlord will not be required to provide an aid which has a general purpose need.

A landlord would not be expected to provide a wheelchair for a tenant who has difficulty walking, as the tenant would need this for their general use, not just for getting around the premises.

The landlord or manager is under a duty to respond to a request from a tenant or prospective tenant, not to anticipate what may be required.

In terms of costs, the landlord or manager can recoup the costs of such work, but this would need to be from all tenants, including the disabled person. Requesting payment only from the disabled person could be considered discriminatory under the 2005 Act.

There is no duty on landlords under the 2005 Act to make adjustments to physical features of the tenant's property, or to any other parts of the landlord's building. Exactly what constitutes a physical feature for this purpose has yet to be finalised within the regulations that will follow the 2005 Act.

## Commonhold associations

Commonhold is a system of freehold ownership applicable to blocks of flats, shops, offices and other multiple occupation premises in England and Wales. A commonhold development consists of interdependent freehold properties, known as commonhold units, and common parts.

Whilst each unit is owned individually, the common parts are owned and managed by a commonhold association. This association is a limited company and only unit owners can be members. There is no landlord and tenant relationship between the unit owners and the commonhold association. To manage the common parts, a commonhold community statement must be established which sets out rules which govern the way in which the commonhold will be managed.

To ensure that disabled people who are unit owners are not discriminated against, the 2005 Act provides that:

- commonhold premises should be subject to the new duties of reasonable adjustment;
- the commonhold association should be treated as though it was a controller of the premises, and that the commonhold units will be treated as premises to let;
- a unit owner will have the same rights to reasonable adjustments as a person to whom the premises are let;

- rules within the commonhold community statement will be treated in the same way as a term of letting.

## Improvements to let dwelling houses

The 2005 Act provides a remedy for residential tenants whose land-lords refuse to consent to the tenant making improvements that are intended to facilitate the tenant's enjoyment of the property, or the enjoyment of any disabled person who lawfully occupies the property. Where a landlord unreasonably withholds consent in these circumstances, consent is deemed to have been given.

> Examples given in the Code of Practice of types of improvements include a disabled person with a mobility impairment needing a grab rail to help them move about the premises, and a disabled woman with arthritis wanting to install easy-to-use controls for her central heating system.

This provision does not apply to protected tenancies or statutory tenancies, as similar rights already apply by virtue of the Housing Acts.

The 2005 Act also makes provision for the Disability Rights Commission (DRC) to make arrangements to provide conciliation services in relation to a dispute concerning the question of whether it is reasonable for a landlord to withhold his consent to the making of a relevant improvement to a dwelling house.

The DRC is preparing a new code of practice giving practical guidance to landlords and tenants with regard to consent to the making of relevant adjustments and circumstances in which a landlord's refusal of consent to an improvement is unreasonable.

## Advertising

Since October 2004, it has been illegal under the DDA 1995 for a company to place a discriminating advertisement, one that might suggest, for example, that the company does not wish people with a disability to apply for the post.

Under the 2005 Act, it is now also against the law for publishers to print discriminatory advertisements. However, publishers may be able to defend printing a discriminatory advertisement if they can show that the person placing it had stated that it was not unlawful, and it was reasonable for them (the publishers) to rely on that statement.

## Councillors

Under the 2005 Act, an authority has a duty not to discriminate against a disabled councillor:

- in the opportunities it affords the councillor for receiving training or other benefits (including goods, facilities and services provided to the councillor);
- by refusing to afford, or by deliberately not affording, the councillor such opportunities;
- by subjecting the councillor to any other detriment.

These duties apply to the general work undertaken by the councillor, but do not extend to activities brought about by essentially political decisions, such as appointments to serve on committees or to a position on the council's executive.

In essence, a local authority could be regarded as discriminating against a disabled councillor where:

- for a reason related to the councillor's disability, it treats him or her less favourably than non-disabled councillors, and for reasons that cannot be justified;
- it fails to comply with a duty to make reasonable adjustments for that councillor.

It is suggested that there are about 109 000 councillors in Great Britain, of whom about 13% self-report that they are disabled with a disability that might meet the definition of a disabled person under the DDA 1995. However, there was no duty placed on a council by the DDA 1995 not to discriminate against disabled councillors. The DDA 2005 fills this loophole.

The duty to make reasonable adjustments requires a local authority to take reasonable steps to change policies, practices and procedures, or to alter physical features of buildings that place a disabled councillor at a substantial disadvantage in comparison with non-disabled councillors. These duties are similar to the existing duties on employers under Part 2 of the DDA 1995.

## Transport

The 2005 Act extends the scope of the DDA to cover discrimination in relation to transport. At present, transport infrastructure is covered by the DDA , and regulations made under the DDA set out accessibility requirements for new trains, taxis and buses. However, the DDA does not apply to the management or operation of transport services. The 2005 Act amends the DDA to include a regulation making power to enable the Secretary of State to lift the exemption in respect of transport providers operating certain types of vehicles.

The Disability Discrimination (Transport Vehicles) Regulations 2006 have been made under this power. The 2006 Regulations lift the exemption for the providers of transport who provide such services through the use of specified vehicles and apply certain provisions of Part 3 of the DDA to such providers. The extent to which the exemption is lifted depends on the type of service. The 2006 Regulations cover buses, coaches, private hire vehicles and taxis.

> Under the 1995 Act, a wheelchair user has no redress if a bus driver fails to park an accessible bus close enough to the kerb to allow wheelchair access onto the bus. Under the 2006 Regulations, the bus company can be treated as a service provider with duties under Part 3 of the DDA covering issues such as boarding, travelling and alighting.

## Question and reply procedure

Section 56 of the DDA 1995 is entirely replaced by the 2005 Act. That section sets out a framework for a questions and reply

**Figure 3.6** Lifts can help everyone access facilities.

procedure which may be used by complainants in deciding whether to bring a claim under Part 2 of the DDA 1995. The revised section extends that framework so that it will also apply to claims brought under Part 3 of the DDA 1995.

## Implementation

The 2005 Act comes into force at various stages. The current programme for implementation runs from December 2005 to December 2006.

## Codes of Practice

Codes of Practice have been published, or are being prepared, to cover the new duties under the 2005 Act. At the time of writing, there is a new Code of Practice covering the Disability Equality Duty and draft codes on transport and Part 3 of the Act.

## The Building Regulations

The Building Regulations provide functional requirements for building design and construction. They exist to ensure the health and safety of people in and around all types of buildings and also provide for energy conservation and access. The Regulations are made under powers provided in the Building Act 1984, and apply in England and Wales. The current edition of the regulations is The Building Regulations 2000 (as amended). The Building Regulations 2000 and the Approved Documents do not apply to Scotland. Scotland has its own set of relevant laws, the Building Standards (Scotland) Regulations 1981 and the Building Standards and Procedures (Amendment) (Scotland) Regulations 1999.

The requirements with which building work must comply are contained in a schedule (Schedule 1) to the Building Regulations and are grouped under 14 parts. The parts deal with individual aspects of building design and construction ranging from structural matters, fire safety, and energy conservation to hygiene, sound insulation, and access to and use of buildings. The requirements within each part set out the broad objectives or functions which the individual aspects of the building design and construction must set out to achieve.

The requirements of the Building Regulations that relate to access are mainly covered in Part M – Access to and use of buildings, and Part B – Fire safety. Part K contains general guidance on stair and ramp design; however, as the 2004 edition of Approved Document M reflects more recent guidance on these matters it takes preference over Approved Document K where it may appear to conflict.

## The Approved Documents

Guidance on how to comply with the requirements in the Building Regulations is given in a series of Approved Documents, one for each Part. Each of the documents gives general guidance on performance of building work and materials and practical examples and solutions on how to achieve compliance. It is not mandatory to comply with this guidance; other methods of construction or design may be equally acceptable provided the Building Regulation requirements are met.

The Approved Documents can be found on the website of the Department for Communities and Local Government (www.communities.gov.uk).

## Part M – Access to and use of buildings

Part M of the Building Regulations relates to access to and use of buildings. It applies to new buildings and some extensions, material alterations and changes of use. It is intended to ensure that people, regardless of disability, age or gender, can gain access to and within buildings and use their facilities, both as visitors and as people who live and work in them, and use sanitary conveniences in the principal storey of a new dwelling. The requirements of Part M are as set out below.

**Access and use**

**M1**   Reasonable provision shall be made for people to:

- gain access to; and
- use the building and its facilities.

The requirements of this part do not apply to:

- an extension of or material alteration of a dwelling; or
- any part of a building which is used solely to enable the building or any service or fitting in the building to be inspected, maintained or repaired.

**Access to extensions to buildings other than dwellings**

**M2**   Suitable independent access shall be provided to the extension where reasonably practicable.
   Requirement M2 does not apply where suitable access to the extension is provided through the building that is extended.

**Sanitary conveniences in extensions to buildings other than dwellings**

**M3**   If sanitary conveniences are provided in any building that is to be extended, reasonable provision shall be made within the extension for sanitary conveniences.

Requirement M3 does not apply where there is reasonable provision for sanitary conveniences elsewhere in the building, such that people occupied in, or otherwise having occasion to enter, the extension can gain access to and use those sanitary conveniences.

### Sanitary conveniences in dwellings

**M4**  Reasonable provision shall be made in the entrance storey for sanitary conveniences, or where the entrance storey contains no habitable rooms, reasonable provision for sanitary conveniences shall be made in either the entrance storey or principal storey. (Entrance storey is defined as the storey that contains the principal entrance. Principal storey is the storey nearest to the entrance storey which contains a habitable room, or if there are two such storeys equally near, either such storey.)

## Application of Part M    The requirements apply if:

- a non-domestic building or a dwelling is newly erected;
- an existing non-domestic building is extended, or undergoes a material alteration; or
- an existing building or part of an existing building undergoes a material change of use to a hotel or boarding house, institution, public building or shop.

Part M also applies to features outside a building which are needed to provide access to the building from the edge of the site and from car parking within the site.

### Approved Document M    Approved Document M (AD M) gives guidance on Part M of the Building Regulations. The document sets out a number of objectives to be met, covers design considerations and gives technical details of design solutions. These solutions, called provisions in the document, show one way in which the requirements might be met, though alternative solutions may well be acceptable provided the overall objective is met.

Approved Document M deals with the means of access to and into buildings other than dwellings, circulation inside such buildings, and facilities and sanitary accommodation. With regard to dwellings the document covers access to and into dwellings, circulation within the entrance storey, accessible switches and socket outlets and WC provision in the entrance storey.

> The provisions given in Approved Document M do not show the only way of meeting the requirements, they merely illustrate one way and there is no obligation to adopt any of them. Alternative solutions may well be acceptable provided the overall objective is met.

Following the publication of BS 8300: 2001 Design of buildings and their approaches to meet the needs of disabled people – Code of Practice, the Approved Document was revised and reissued as Approved Document M, 2004 edition. This new edition takes account of many of the recommendations in BS 8300. Further revisions to the guidance given in AD M have been made since the publication of the 2004 edition and are listed on the website www.communities.gov.uk under Building Regulations, in the Approved Document M Frequently Asked Questions (FAQ) pages. At the time of writing, the topics covered in the FAQ include the relationship of BS 8300 and AD M, light reflectance values, opening/closing force of doors and handrail dimensions.

**Access statements**    The Approved Document includes information on access statements and recommends that an access statement should be provided with Building Regulation applications. It notes that such a statement might record the intention of the applicant to comply, where appropriate, with the guidance in Approved Document M. Where an applicant wishes to depart from the guidance either to achieve a better solution using new technologies, to provide a more convenient solution, or to address the constraints of an existing building, the statement can be used to set out the reasons for departing from the guidance and the rationale for the design approach adopted. In the case of extensions and material changes of use of buildings, and particularly in the case of historic buildings, an access statement can also be used to propose compensatory measures where full access proves to be impracticable or unreasonable.

Information on the role of access statements, and the issues that should be included at various stages of a project, is given in Chapter 1. Guidance is also available on the Disability Rights Commission website (www.drc-gb.org) under Employers and Services.

## Building Regulations and the Disability Discrimination Act (DDA)

The duty under Part 3 of the DDA to make reasonable adjustments to physical features of buildings can be affected by Building Regulation compliance. Where the physical features of a building met the requirements of Part M (or its equivalent in Northern Ireland or Scotland) at the time of its construction, and continue to meet them, a service provider may not have to make any further adjustment to those features. This might apply, for example, to the width of a corridor; however, the service provider might still need to alter other aspects of the corridor such as a floor finish that impedes access.

This partial exemption to the duties under Part 3 of the Act is only available for a period of 10 years from the date when a feature was constructed. The exemption does not apply to employers under Part 2.

---

It would be unfortunate if designers opted for the simple solution of following the guidance in Approved Document M in every case, in order to be sure of gaining future exemption, rather than developing more creative solutions to access issues that may be more suitable for the particular building or circumstance.

It must also be remembered that the exemption only applies to those elements of a building to which Part M applies. Therefore, items such as floor finishes, lighting, acoustics, etc., may not be subject to the exemption.

## Part B – Fire safety

Part B of the Building Regulations applies to all construction, including new-build, refurbishment, extensions and alterations and sets out the requirements for fire safety. Approved Document B gives guidance on meeting these requirements and includes information on fire alarm and detection systems, escape provision in various building types, fire spread and access and facilities for the fire service. With regard to means of escape for disabled people the document states:

'it may not be necessary to incorporate special structural measures to aid means of escape for the disabled. Management arrangements to provide assisted escape may be all that is necessary.'

The Approved Document makes reference to BS 5588, which gives detailed information on the design, construction and use of buildings.

**Figure 3.7** Evacuation lifts make emergency egress easier in multi-storey buildings.

## BS 5588 Fire precautions in the design, construction and use of buildings

BS 5588 covers different building types and elements of buildings. It is divided into a number of parts and BS 5588-8 covers means of escape for disabled people. It introduces the concepts of refuges, which are designated safe areas for disabled people to wait in the event of a fire, and the use of evacuation lifts and stresses the need for effective management of the evacuation. Further information on emergency evacuation is given in Chapter 4.

## BS 8300:2001 Design of buildings and their approaches to meet the needs of disabled people – Code of Practice

BS 8300:2001 is an amalgamation and updating of BS 5619:1978 and BS 5810:1979, and gives detailed guidance on good practice in the design of domestic and non-domestic buildings. Importantly, the guidance also draws on research, commissioned by the Department of the Environment, Transport and the Regions in 1997 and 2001, into the access needs of disabled people. The research looked into issues such as reach ranges and space requirements in order to assess the capabilities and needs of people in relation to the use of buildings. The guidance incorporates the research findings and gives detailed design recommendations set in context by a commentary explaining user needs.

BS 8300:2001 contains sections covering building elements as well as particular building types and the guidance given takes account of a wide range of needs. The British Standard gives recommendations on car parking, access routes to and around buildings, entrances and interiors, horizontal and vertical circulation, surfaces and communication aids, facilities in buildings, assembly areas, individual rooms and building types.

The BS was revised in 2005 and changes made to areas of guidance including visual contrast, doors, handrails, tactile paving, stairs, floor surfaces, manifestation and WC fittings.

It is likely that the guidance given in the British Standard will be taken into account when considering 'reasonable provision' in relation to the Disability Discrimination Act.

## BS 7000-6:2005 Design management systems. Managing inclusive design

BS 7000-6:2005 covers the management of inclusive design, not the practice, and sets out a comprehensive framework for introducing a professional approach to inclusive design into organisations. The two main sections contain guidance at the organisation and project levels respectively.

Issues clarified include responsibility for inclusive design, and the formulation of a business case for adopting an inclusive approach that is tied closely with an organisation's core objectives, strategies and plans. Guidance is also provided on how current operations and facilities might be reviewed to check their appropriateness, and how experience and best practices elsewhere might be used effectively. Development and marketing strategies are outlined relating to new products and services.

## Planning legislation and guidance

### The planning system

The planning system in England and Wales follows a plan-led system. This involves preparing plans that set out what can be built and where. The system was updated by the Planning and Compulsory Purchase Act in 2004.

The Act established a number of measures intended to make the planning system clearer, faster and more certain. The main provisions of the Act are described here.

- Planning Policy Guidance notes are replaced with Planning Policy Statements, a more streamlined set of government planning policies.
- Structure plans are abolished and strategic planning policy provided instead by Regional Planning Bodies. Local planning authorities will still produce local planning policy but in a new more flexible form – a Local Development Framework, made up of Local Development Documents. These replace Local Plans and Unitary Development Plans.

- Local planning authorities now have wider compulsory purchase powers and compensation will be available to occupiers as well as owners.
- The Act also introduced design and access statements, which would explain and justify the design and access principles and concepts on which a development proposal is based.

In the preparation of development plans and frameworks, the planning authority must take into account any national and regional planning guidance that is relevant at the time. Such guidance is mainly identified in a series of Planning Policy Statements (PPS).

Wales has a Spatial Plan setting out national policies and Local Development Plans for local areas. A new planning bill was introduced in the Scottish Parliament at the end of 2005. It is intended to modernise the planning system in Scotland and introduce a National Planning Framework and a system of Local Development Plans.

## Planning Policy Statements and Guidance Notes

Planning Policy Statements (PPS) replace the old Planning Policy Guidance Notes (PPG) and set out the government's policy on a range of planning issues. PPS are guidance, not law, but all local authorities must have regard of the contents of the statements when drawing up local plans or making decisions on planning applications.

The guidance and statements that relate to access include the following.

**Planning Policy Statement 1 (PPS 1): Delivering sustainable development (2004)**   PPS 1 sets out the overarching planning policies on the delivery of sustainable development through the planning system. These policies complement, but do not replace or override, other national planning policies and should be read in conjunction with other relevant statements of national planning policy. This PPS replaces Planning Policy Guidance Note 1: General Policies and Principles (PPG 1 1997).

**Planning Policy Guidance Note 3 (PPG 3): Housing (1992, revised 2000)**   PPG 3 has as an objective that local planning authorities should plan to meet the housing requirements of the whole community including those in need of affordable and special needs housing.

**Planning Policy Statement 6 (PPS 6): Planning for Town Centres (2005)**   PPS 6 sets out the Government's key objectives for town centres including planning for the growth and development of existing centres; promoting and enhancing existing centres, by focusing development in such centres; and encouraging a wide range of services in a good environment, accessible to all. This Planning Policy Statement replaces Revised Planning Policy Guidance Note 6: Town Centres and Retail Developments (PPG 6 1996)

**Planning Policy Statement 11 (PPS 11): Regional Spatial Strategies (2004)**   PPS 11 sets out the procedural policy on the nature of Regional Spatial Strategies and focuses on what should happen in preparing revisions to them and explains how this relates to the Act and associated regulations.

**Planning Policy Statement 12 (PPS 12): Local Development Frameworks (2004)**   PPG 12 states that local planning authorities, in preparing development plans, should consider the relationship of planning policies and proposals to social needs and problems, including their likely impact on different groups in the population, such as disabled people and others.

**Planning Policy Guidance Note 13 (PPG 13): Transport (2001)**   PPG 13 notes that local authorities, developers and transport providers should work together to seek to meet the accessibility needs of disabled people in all developments. It notes that local authorities, in developing and implementing policies on parking, should require developers to provide designated parking spaces for disabled people in accordance with current good practice.

**Planning Policy Guidance Note 15 (PPG 15): Planning and the Historic Environment (1994)**    PPG 15 states that it is important in principle that disabled people should have dignified, easy access to and within historic buildings. It goes on to say that it should normally be possible to plan suitable access without compromising a building's special interest.

**Planning Policy Guidance Note 17 (PPG 17): Planning for Open Space, Sport and Recreation (2002)**    PPG 17 states that local authorities should take account of the mobility needs of the local population and should ensure that facilities are accessible for disabled people.

**Design and access statements**    The Planning and Compulsory Purchase Act 2004 introduced a requirement, taking effect from August 2006, to submit a design and access statement with applications for planning permission and listed building consent, subject to certain limited exceptions. This is intended to demonstrate a commitment to take the issue of inclusive design seriously at the earliest stages of a project.

The exact form of the access statement will depend on the size, nature and complexity of the scheme. The information that should be included in the statement is listed in Chapter 1 in the section on Access statements. In the case of existing buildings, particularly historic buildings, such a statement enables a designer or developer to identify the constraints posed by the existing structure and its immediate environment and to explain how these have been overcome.

Information on access statements is also included in the section of this chapter on Part M of the Building Regulations.

## Planning guidance

**Planning and Access for Disabled People – a good practice guide (ODPM 2003)**    The guide addresses the need for the planning system to enhance and enforce inclusive design provisions by those applying for planning consent. The guide describes how all those involved in the planning process can play their part in delivering a physical environment that can be used by everyone and explains the respective roles of the planning system, Building Regulations and the DDA.

Recommendations of the Guide include the following:

- There should be an awareness of inclusive design and inclusive design principles should underpin planning policy. Non-inclusive applications should be rejected and local supplementary guidance should be developed. Conditions should be applied where appropriate.
- Applicants should be encouraged to consider access issues through pre-application discussion. Application forms should be amended to prompt thinking about access and access statements should be required.
- Officers should be trained in access issues and a role for the Royal Town Planning Institute is envisaged in this regard. It is suggested that local authorities should consider appointing an access officer if they do not have one. There should be a sharing of experiences and knowledge, as within the organisation of the Access Association.
- There should be liaison with local people and other statutory functions.

**Greater London Authority (GLA) London Plan**   The Greater London Authority (GLA) London Plan is a spatial development strategy, which covers sustainability and social inclusion. The key aspects of the plan are as follows:

- Creating an inclusive environment: developments should meet the highest standards of accessibility and inclusion. Boroughs should adopt the principles of inclusive design and an access statement should accompany proposals.
- Principles of inclusive design: developments should be used by as many people as possible, without undue effort, separation or special treatment. Developments should offer freedom to choose and the ability to participate equally in

mainstream activities. Developments should value diversity and difference.
- Housing choices: new housing developments should offer a range of housing choices in terms of the mix of housing sizes and types, taking into account the housing requirements of different groups such as students, older people and families with children. All new housing should be to lifetime homes standards, i.e. houses that can be adapted to the changing needs of their residents. Some 10% of new housing must be designed to wheelchair-accessible standards or easily adapted for residents who are wheelchair users. The GLA is looking at the possibility of creating a register of accessible housing stock.

Supplementary planning guidance entitled Accessible London: Achieving an Inclusive Environment was published at the same time as the London Plan. This explains the principles of inclusive design and the social model of disability, gives planners advice and good practice points, offers designers advice and guidance, and identifies legislation and national policy guidance.

**Figure 3.8** A change of level at the entrance to a building can be overcome by ramping the pavement.

## Occupier Liability Acts

### Who is an occupier?

The occupier of a premises can be defined as a person who has a:

'sufficient degree of control over premises that he ought to realise that any failure on his part to use care may result in injury to a person coming lawfully there'. (Lord Denning)

The person who is 'coming lawfully there' is defined as a visitor.

### Occupier Liability Act 1957 (OLA 57)

Under the OLA 57, the occupier owes a single common duty of care to all his or her visitors. This common duty of care is a duty to take such care as in all the circumstances of the case is reasonable to see that the visitor will be reasonably safe in using the premises when he or she is invited or permitted by the occupier to be there.

In general, the standard of care that can be expected of an occupier is the same as that in an ordinary action of negligence. Therefore, whilst the occupier would not be expected to guard against improbable or unlikely events, he or she must do sufficient to exercise the common duty of care described above. In addition, it is not the premises but the visitor who must be made reasonably safe, and the precautions needed to fulfil this duty will vary according to the particular visitor.

Importantly, where a landlord retains control of the access to premises or to the common parts of a property, he or she is treated as the occupier and thereby owes the common duty of care to the tenants, their families and their visitors.

Whilst an occupier may discharge his or her duty to a visitor by giving a warning of any danger that may exist, the warning may not be taken as absolving the occupier unless in 'all the circumstances' it was enough to enable the visitor to be reasonably safe. The simple presence of a warning does not necessarily suffice.

## Occupier Liability Act 1984 (OLA 84)

Under the OLA 84, an occupier may owe a duty to persons other than his visitors, often referred to as non-visitors. This may include, for example, trespassers, people who enter the land or the area occupied in the lawful pursuance of their job or people lawfully exercising a private right of way. The duty is to take such care as is reasonable in all the circumstances of the case to see that the 'non-visitor does not suffer injury on the premises because of a danger that may exist there'.

What constitutes reasonable care will vary with circumstances. These varying circumstances might include the way the building or space was entered, the age of the person entering, the type and nature of the premises, the extent of the risk and the cost of carrying out precautionary work.

## Relationship of the Occupier Liability Acts to inclusive design and access management

Employers, service providers and others may well have responsibilities, relating to accessibility, under the Occupier Liability Acts, as well as under the DDA. For example, in existing buildings it is common to find an accessible WC that is not provided with an emergency alarm call. The DDA identifies that it should not be unreasonably difficult to use a service – but is the lack of an alarm in an accessible WC making that WC any more difficult to use than the general provision WCs? In most cases it could be argued that to specify the provision of an alarm could be seen as a reasonable provision, the limited cost and the inconvenience of doing so being unlikely to make such an action unreasonable for most service providers.

As occupiers, the service provider will owe a duty of care to visitors 'to take such care as in all the circumstances of the case is reasonable to see that the visitor will be reasonably safe in using the premises'.

With regard to the use of an accessible WC facility, it is known, for example, that disabled people can experience some difficulty, and even danger, when transferring between the wheelchair and the WC. If they fall and are unable to call for assistance, they may be in the toilet for some time before being discovered. What must be considered in each individual case is whether the occupier is taking such care as 'in all the circumstances of the case' is reasonable to ensure that visitors are safe when using the premises.

There are several examples within the built environment to which this could be applied. For example, it could be argued that slippery, shiny floor finishes do not necessarily discriminate against disabled people because all users experience difficulties when using them. However, disabled people may certainly find the use of such floors more difficult, restrictive and dangerous than other people. It could be argued that a service provider needs to take into account when considering 'all the circumstances of the case' that the needs of disabled people using his or her service, who might be more vulnerable to slipping and falling, are greater than those of other people and should be addressed accordingly.

The examples given above are by no means the only areas that may need to be considered. Each issue should be considered on its merits. The duty owed 'in all the circumstances of the case' to disabled people who may be non-visitors under the OLA 84 may also be different to that owed to others – especially if a difference in the level of ability could be foreseen.

In that respect, the recommendations made to address some issues identified in an access audit may well be based upon the responsibilities of the service provider or employer under legislation other than the DDA (e.g. OLA, Health and Safety) and the audit report should identify the items that relate to either discrimination or minimum legal management standards.

> An access audit, and the recommendations which arise from it, should clearly identify those issues which relate to discrimination under the DDA and those issues which relate to appropriate management practices by an occupier or employer under other legislation.

# 4 Design criteria

## Introduction

Access to buildings and environments, and the services they house, is easier for everyone if certain basic criteria are met. These criteria cover issues that affect all building users, not just specific groups of people.

It is not necessary to separate the needs of a wheelchair user from those of an ambulant person – both need to be able to find the entrance to a building, enter through the doorway and approach the reception desk, both may need to use a lavatory or a car park. If people are divided into groups based on differing needs, it is apparent that the areas of overlap far exceed the specific requirements for each group. The design guidance given here is intended to cover the needs of as wide a range of users as possible.

This approach does not deny that there are specific areas where particular assistance can be provided. Hearing enhancement systems, such as induction loops, or the provision of information in Braille, are useful to certain building users. Specific provisions that meet particular needs should be part of inclusive design.

The guidance given here can be used when designing new buildings or taken as a standard to assess and improve existing buildings. However, it is important that it is seen in context – inclusive design is not simply the application of a set of criteria. The effective implementation of much of the guidance depends upon management understanding and input. To be effective, inclusive design should be seen as an approach that is an integral part of the design process and continues throughout the life of a building or environment. Issues of management, maintenance and building use will affect whether a good level of access, and inclusiveness, is achieved and is sustained in use.

The list of design criteria that follows is not exhaustive – it is intended to cover those areas that most often cause problems for users. Sources of greater detail, where appropriate, are noted in the text and listed in Appendix B.

## External environment

### Car parking

Car parking or setting down are often the first activities that take place on arrival at a public, commercial building or employment building and can have a great effect on ease of access. Issues such as signs, travel distances from car park to entrance and design of external routes affect everyone, not just disabled people. Depending on the building use, consideration should be given to providing priority parking spaces for anyone who needs to park nearer the entrance, for example parent and child parking, in addition to designated spaces for disabled people.

- Car parking should be provided close to the entrance to the building and, especially on sloping sites, designated parking provision for disabled people should be at the same level as the entrance.
- Designated car parking provision should be signposted from the entrance to the car park and the bays clearly identified.
- The number of designated parking spaces should be appropriate for the type and use of building.

**Figure 4.1** Car park showing excellent use of signage, ground markings and pedestrian routes.

- Designated parking spaces should be within 50 m of the principal entrance to the building; where the route is covered this could be increased up to 100 m maximum.
- Bays should be of sufficient size to allow doors and boot lids to be fully opened and to allow drivers and passengers to transfer to a wheelchair. A single accessible bay should be a minimum of 4800 mm long by 3600 mm wide. If a bank of bays is provided, each bay should be at least 4800 mm long by 2400 mm wide with an additional 1200 mm transfer zone between bays. A 1200 mm wide safety zone is required for boot access and use of rear hoists.

Where there is insufficient space to make all disabled parking bays long enough to allow for rear exit and loading, a marked-out pedestrian route on the road behind the parking spaces can double up as loading space.

**Figure 4.2** Parking bay with adequate room for both side and rear exit and entry to allow easy use. Although the rear exit and entry area is not marked, it can clearly be achieved without encroaching into the vehicle route.

- Pedestrian routes in car parks should be clearly defined.
- Where there are kerbs between parking areas, transfer areas and routes to the building, they should be dropped to allow easy passage for wheelchair users, with tactile paving provided at all road crossing points.
- The car park surface should be smooth and even.
- Designated parking for disabled people in multi-storey car parks should be at the same level as the principal accessible entrance to the building or the main access route to and from the car park. There should be signs indicating the accessible route to ticket machines, lifts and exits and, where appropriate, the building that is being visited.
- Where there are ticket machines, coin- or card-operated barriers or other controls, these should be at an appropriate height and designed to allow easy use by everyone.
- It is important that management procedures are in place, and in use, to ensure that other motorists do not use the bays designated for disabled people to use.

**Figure 4.3** Good clear signage, correct drainage, and firm non-slip surfaces are essential. Routes between parking areas should be clear and well defined; bollards can prevent encroachment.

**Figure 4.4** Parking is at same level as entrance to shopping area with a clearly defined route.

Recommended numbers of designated spaces for disabled people are given in Inclusive Mobility as follows:

- for car parks associated with existing employment premises – 2% of the total capacity, with a minimum of one space (this figure does not include spaces for disabled employees);
- for car parks associated with new employment premises – 5% of the total parking capacity (to include both employees and visitors);
- for car parks associated with shopping areas, leisure or recreational facilities and places open to the general public – a minimum of one space for each employee who is a disabled motorist, plus 6% of the total capacity for visiting disabled motorists.

The number of designated spaces may need to be greater at buildings that specialise in accommodating groups of disabled people, such as some hotels and sports stadia.

## Setting down

A setting down point is useful for people arriving by car, taxi or dial-a-ride bus.

- A clearly sign-posted setting down point on a level surface close to the main entrance of the building should be provided, with a shelter if possible.

It is essential to ensure that dropping off points are properly signed and managed so that they are not used for other 'quick activities' such as the delivery of goods.

## External routes

External routes around buildings should be designed to allow easy, unobstructed access for everyone. Routes should be clearly

**Figure 4.5** Setting down and pick-up points should be clearly marked with dropped kerbs. Care should be taken to ensure bollards do not obstruct routes.

**Figure 4.6** Seating can be useful on longer routes. Armrests can help people when sitting or standing.

defined, wide enough for all users, free from hazards and have firm, even, slip-resistant surfaces.

**Surfaces**    Uneven surfaces, loose material such as gravel and wide joints between paving units can all cause problems for people using external routes. For wheelchair users, people with visual impairments and people who are unsteady on their feet, such surfaces can be hazardous or prevent use of the route.

- Surfaces should be firm, even and consistent and have a slip-resistant finish in all weather conditions.
- The material used to form the path should be capable of withstanding the loads and volume of traffic it will carry.
- Path surfaces containing grass, unless supported by a suitable reinforced mesh, gravel or deeply ridged concrete sets should be avoided.
- Joints between paving units should not exceed 10 mm in width and 5 mm in depth.

**Figure 4.7**  Good surfaces and level entrances are necessary, but management control of potential obstructions is also required.

- The edges of paths should be provided with some method of assisting blind or partially sighted users, for example, a raised kerb or tapping rail, though care should be taken to ensure that this does not represent a tripping hazard for other users.
- Pedestrian and vehicular routes should be clearly distinguished using texture, colour or a small change in level, with dropped kerbs where appropriate.
- Changes in texture and profile of paving can be used to give information to pedestrians. A surface that is uncomfortable to walk on can be used to steer people away from a hazard or a route across a large open space can be identified by a difference in surface.

An accessible route can be formed by laying a smooth path of stone or concrete paving across an existing uneven surface, such as cobbles or gravel.

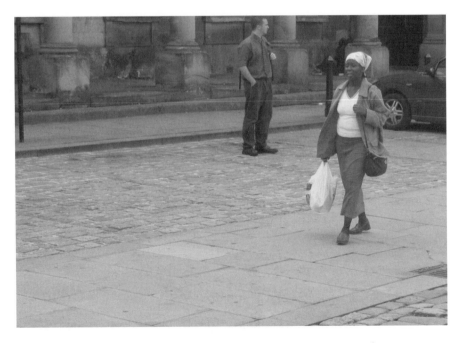

**Figure 4.8** A smooth path can be laid across an uneven surface to provide an accessible route.

**Tactile paving** There are a number of specific profiles of paving that have been developed to give particular information to pedestrians.

- The modified blister is used externally at a dropped kerb or raised road surface to indicate the edge of the footway and the start of the carriageway.
- Corduroy paving, which has a half-rod-shaped profile in a ribbed pattern, is used to provide a hazard warning. Guidance in Approved Document M states that this should be used at the top and bottom of external flights of steps and at intermediate landings where there is access onto the landing other than from the steps (see *External steps and stairs*).
- A flat-topped ribbed profile is used to denote a guidance path. This could be used in a large open space such as a pedestrian precinct.

There are also specific profiles for use at platform edges and on segregated paths for cyclists and pedestrians. Detailed information on tactile paving is given in Guidance on the Use of Tactile Paving Surfaces (DTLR 1999).

> Where tactile paving is used it should be of the correct profile, colour and hardness to give the appropriate message. For people who rely on tactile clues to gain information about the environment, being given the wrong information is often much worse than being given no information at all. If there is no information, they will be alert to potential problems; incorrect information could give a false sense of security and be potentially dangerous.

**Path width and gradient** The width of paths should be adequate to meet the needs of all users. People using wheelchairs, pushing buggies or using walking aids should be able to pass each other easily. On narrower paths passing places should be provided.

**Figure 4.9** A good approach to a building can greatly enhance people's perception of it as well as its accessibility.

- The recommended minimum width for paths is 1200 mm, though 1500 mm is preferred. A width of 1800 mm will allow wheelchairs and pushchairs to pass each other.
- Path gradient should be less than 1 in 20. A path with a gradient of 1 in 20 or greater should be treated as a ramp with appropriate handrails and landings.
- The cross fall on a path is also important, especially for people using wheelchairs, and should not exceed 1 in 50.

A dropped kerb can allow a blind or partially sighted person to leave the pavement unknowingly; tactile paving should always be provided to give information about the lack of a kerb and the potential danger ahead.

**Figure 4.10** A barrier to mobility?

**Changes of direction**   Care should be taken at junctions and corners of paths to ensure that any change of direction can be undertaken easily, safely and with minimum effort from the user. Ambulant disabled people, wheelchair and guide dog users and those pushing prams or buggies will have certain width requirements in negotiating changes of direction and these must be allowed for in any path design.

- Wherever possible corners at changes in direction should be splayed or rounded.

**Gratings**   Drainage gratings can cause tripping, slipping and trap wheelchair wheels, ends of sticks, crutches and the heels of shoes. Where feasible they should be positioned off routes. If they are located within paths, they should be flush with the surrounding surface.

- Slots in grating should be less that 13 mm wide and set at right angles to the direction of travel.
- Circular holes should not exceed 18 mm diameter.

**Figure 4.11** Potential tripping hazards should be highlighted using visual contrast.

- Dished channels can cause tripping and should not be provided on access routes. Where a drainage channel is incorporated at a dropped kerb, there should be a flat plate across the channel for the length of the dropped section.

**Dropped kerbs**    At pedestrian crossing points and other places where level access is required between path and a carriageway, for example in a car park, there should be a dropped kerb.

- The width of the dropped section should be at least 1200 mm, though 2000 mm is preferred.
- Gradients of paving at dropped kerbs should not exceed 1 in 15.
- It is very important to provide the correct profile, colour and layout of tactile paving to give the appropriate information at road crossings. See Guidance on the Use of Tactile Paving Surfaces (DTLR 1999).

**Street furniture**    Street furniture such as litterbins, signposts, bollards and seating should be carefully designed and placed so as not to obstruct routes or restrict widths and should be clearly visible. Items could be grouped and clear routes identified by textural changes in paving.

- Paths should be kept clear of obstructions at ground level, such as litterbins or planters, or any projections into the walking zone such as projecting signs or overhanging tree branches.
- Bollards should be a minimum of 1000 mm high and adequately contrasted with the background against which they will be viewed.

The visibility of potential obstacles is important to many people. People who are deaf or hard of hearing and who are talking and looking at a companion, or communicating using lip reading or signing, will be relying on their peripheral vision to identify obstacles. Appropriate visual contrast of potential obstacles is essential for them, just as it is for a person with a visual impairment or anyone who is simply walking along not paying attention.

**Figure 4.12** Projections into the walking zone can be very dangerous for all people, but especially people with visual impairments. Projections should be avoided, or at least properly protected, at all times.

**Figure 4.13** Seating should be located where it does not obstruct routes and should be clearly visible.

**Handrails**    Handrails should be provided at changes of level, or as guardings, and can be used to guide people away from obstructions in the walking zone.

**Lighting**    Wherever possible, all external routes should be well illuminated, without strong shadows and dark areas.

- Changes of level and other potential hazards should be well lit.
- Lighting should not give glare or cross shadows, particularly around potential hazards such as steps or ramps.
- Light sources should not reduce colour definition which has been introduced to provide information or identify hazards.

> To be effective, external lighting needs regular maintenance. Fittings should be kept clean to maximise available light, and bulbs and fittings swiftly replaced when damaged or broken.

## External ramps

The provision of appropriately designed, constructed and managed ramps is of importance to all users, but especially those using wheelchairs, pushing buggies or trolleys, and people using walking frames.

> Ramps should only be considered where it is necessary to address unavoidable changes in level and never used simply to overcome changes of level that could have been avoided by good, thoughtful design.

Ramps that are long and steep may cause difficulties, especially for people using wheelchairs. A wheelchair user or companion pushing the wheelchair might not have sufficient strength to travel up a steep gradient or, importantly, to control the journey down. Steep gradients, especially short steep gradients such as those found at doorways and kerbs, can also cause wheelchairs to tip up backwards when going up and increase the danger of a wheelchair user falling forwards when coming down.

Landings are needed as resting places, but travel along long ramps can become tiring even with landings. It is the overall length of travel on the ramp that is important, not the number of places available to allow someone to rest. Ramps should be designed to appropriate gradients, but with the overall length kept to an absolute minimum.

Ramps that cut across stairs, resulting in tapered risers, can be hazardous for people using the stairs and the ramp and should be avoided.

> Some people prefer to use steps rather than a ramp. Steps allow people to rest with their feet on a level surface, rather than a sloping one that can cause pain in the ankles for older people or those with arthritis. Some visually impaired people also prefer to use steps because they give reference points, which can assist with mobility and orientation.

**Figure 4.14** A gently sloping ramp provides access and, in this case, also provides a route over the gravel surface.

- Ramps with a gradient of 1 in 20 or steeper should always be accompanied by steps.
- Travel along ramps can become tiring and so no section of ramp should exceed 10 m in length or 500 mm in rise.
- A series of ramps to a building should not rise in total more than 2 m; beyond this rise an alternative means of vertical travel, such as a lift, should be considered.

**Gradient**  A ramped approach should have the lowest practical gradient:

- 1 in 20 is considered desirable;
- 1 in 15 is acceptable;
- 1 in 12 is the absolute maximum. A gradient of 1 in 12 may be too steep for some wheelchair users and will prevent them from accessing a building. Egress on a 1 in 12 gradient may be difficult to achieve safely.

BS 8300 and Approved Document M give guidance on ramp gradients.

**Figure 4.15** A sensitive addition to increase access to a historic building.

**Figure 4.16** A ramp with a gradient of 1 in 12 may be too steep for people to use easily and conveniently.

**Width**    The minimum surface width of a ramp, as given by Approved Document M, is 1500 mm.

- If the width is less than 1800 mm, two wheelchair users will not be able to pass. Where this occurs there should be a clear unobstructed view along the length of the ramp to ensure that wheelchair users know they can complete their travel without having to reverse up or down the slope.
- Ramps of the minimum width should not exceed 5 m in length, and even then they are not suitable for heavy traffic. Passing places should be incorporated at landings if it is not possible to provide a wider ramp.

---

Reversing up or down a slope, for whatever reason, is a dangerous, often impossible, manoeuvre for a wheelchair user. The need to do it should be avoided in all possible circumstances – and it can be with careful thought and good design.

---

## Landings

- Resting places, in the form of level landings, should be provided along the length of the ramp as follows: every 5 m for a gradient of 1 in 15 and every 10 m for a gradient of 1 in 20. Ramps with a gradient of 1 in 12 should not exceed 2 m in length.
- Intermediate landings should be at least 1500 mm long. Landings of 1800 mm by 1800 mm could also act as passing places.
- Level landings should also be provided at the top and bottom of each ramp, and at changes of direction. The landings at the top and bottom should be a minimum of 1200 mm long and clear of any door swing.
- Unless under cover, a landing should have a cross fall not exceeding 1 in 50 to help drain surface water. If kerbs or upstands prevent water run-off, drainage holes should be provided. Care should be taken to ensure that their size and

position do not endanger ramp users. Slots should run at right angles to the direction of traffic.

## Surfaces

- Surfaces should be smooth, firm, slip resistant even when wet, and easy to maintain.
- To alert people with visual impairments to the presence of a ramp, the landing areas should contrast visually with the sloping sections.
- If different surfaces are used for ramps, landings and approach paths, it is important that the coefficients of friction are similar to minimise risk of stumbling.

---

A corduroy pattern tactile warning surface should not be used at the top or bottom of ramps. This surface is intended for use at steps and may cause confusion, or even be potentially dangerous, if used incorrectly.

---

**Handrails**   Usually wheelchair users will not require a handrail on a ramp. However, in adverse weather conditions or if the ramp is long and steep, handrails may assist wheelchair users in steadying themselves. For ambulant disabled people, especially those with less strength on one side, a handrail is an essential means of support when going up or down a ramp. For visually impaired users, a handrail may be used as a tactile guide that, if extended beyond the end of the ramp, can give useful information about the beginning and the end of the ramp itself.

- Appropriately designed handrails should be provided to both sides of any ramp, with the top edge at a height of 900 mm to 1000 mm above the ramp surface.
- On wide ramps, exceeding 2 m, a central continuous handrail can be provided in addition to side handrails.
- Handrails should be able to be gripped and should extend beyond the start and finish of the ramp by at least 300 m.

**Figure 4.17**  All ramps should have appropriately designed handrails.

For detailed guidance on handrail design see *Internal steps and stairs.*

**Guardrails and kerbs**   Any guardrails or balustrades should be designed with the safety of all users in mind. There should be no risk of wheelchair users catching their feet between balusters. If glazed panels are used, they should be fit for the purpose.

- Where there is no handrail to the open side of a ramp, there should be a raised kerb of at least 100 mm, differentiated from the ramp with visual contrast. This will aid wheelchair users and act as a tapping rail for people using canes.

**Portable or temporary ramps**   Portable or temporary ramps should not be used in new buildings. Where it is not possible to install a permanent ramp in an existing building, for example, within a listed building, the use of a portable or temporary ramp may be necessary. Such a ramp should be designed and used so that it does not constitute a hazard for any users of the building or environment.

The use of a temporary ramp to provide access may be seen as reasonable provision under the DDA in some circumstances. Factors to be taken into account may include the size of the company, the physical practicalities of providing a permanent ramp, the cost and whether the employment opportunity or service could be provided by a reasonable alternative method. There will also be management issues relating to the use of the ramp such as storage, responsibilities for setting up the ramp and offering assistance to users, maintenance and procedures for requesting use, all of which must be dealt with if the ramp is to provide reasonable access.

- A portable or temporary ramp should be well contrasted with its background and well illuminated.
- The surface width of the ramp should be at least 800 mm.
- The surface should be slip resistant and well drained.
- There should be upstands to prevent wheels slipping over the edges of the ramp.
- Gradient should not exceed 1 in 12.

Assistance should always be available for people wishing to use a portable ramp. It is potentially very dangerous to leave a portable ramp in position, at a steep gradient, and allow people to use it without assistance.

**Pavement realignment**   Where there is insufficient space to provide a ramp at the entrance to an existing building, it may be possible to ramp a section of pavement to overcome the change of level. Factors to be considered will include the location of other entrances, the width of the pavement and the resulting height of the kerb. Collaboration with the relevant authorities would be required.

**Figure 4.18** Gently ramping a section of pavement can overcome a change of level at an entrance.

## External steps and stairs

Some ambulant disabled people will find steps easier to negotiate than ramps. The profile of the steps, the surface finishes and the provision of suitably designed handrails is critical.

- Steps should always be provided as an alternative to ramps.
- Handrails should be provided, however short the flight.
- Isolated single steps should be avoided where possible.
- Individual flights should not contain more than 12 risers.
- The width of a stepped access route should be at least 1200 mm.

For detailed guidance on steps and stairs see *Internal steps and stairs.*

**Figure 4.19** Tapered risers can present a serious tripping hazard and should be avoided.

**Handrails**  For many people, handrails are an essential source of information and support. They can warn of the presence of steps, guide and support people using the steps and provide information on the start and finish of a flight and the level reached. The provision of well-designed and positioned handrails is essential for safe, independent use of steps.

Handrails should always be provided to each side of a flight of steps. People may be weaker on one side and require a handrail for support. The division of wider flights into separate channels will allow easier access to handrails when many people are using the stair.

The horizontal extension of a handrail beyond the first and last steps allows an individual to steady or to brace him- or herself before ascending or descending, provides support to ascend the final riser and will signal the start or finish of the flight to people with visual impairments.

For detailed guidance on handrail design see *Internal steps and stairs*.

Steps with handrails to only one side are difficult or impossible for some people to use. Individuals who have had a stroke and have the full use of only one side of their body will need the assistance of a handrail when both ascending and descending the stairs. Guide dog users may not be able to change the side the guide dog operates to allow use of a handrail; people with visual impairments who use a cane for mobility may have similar restrictions.

Equally important are the 300 mm extensions to the top and bottom of handrails, continuous handrails around landings and tactile information to advise people of floor levels. These elements should not be seen as optional – for some people they are the only way that they can obtain the information about their environment to allow them to move around independently, comfortably and safely.

**Figure 4.20** The horizontal extension of a handrail can provide support and also information on the start and finish of the flight of stairs.

**Tactile warning**    There can be a risk of tripping or losing balance, particularly at the head of a flight of steps, and so a warning surface is recommended to alert people to the imminent change of level.

- It is recommended that a corduroy pattern tactile warning surface be provided at the top and bottom of each flight. The surface should extend beyond the width of the flight if practicable. See Guidance on the Use of Tactile Paving Surfaces (DTLR 1999).

For further guidance on steps and stairs see *Internal steps and stairs.*

# Entrances

The entrance to a building will have a significant impact on both the perceived and actual accessibility of the building. The principal entrance should be easily found and used and allow entry by everyone. People should not be segregated on entry by the provision of a separate entrance for those who cannot use the main entrance. There may be existing buildings where an entrance cannot be made accessible and so an alternative means of entry is required, but this approach should be avoided wherever possible and never used in new buildings.

## Entrance design

- The principal entrance to a building should allow access by everyone.
- Entrances should be visible on approach and be able to be distinguished from the façade of the building.
- The location of entrances should relate to external routes and car parking.
- Weather protection should be provided, such as a canopy or recess, unless there are freely accessible automatic doors.
- There should be sufficient manoeuvring space internally and externally to allow everyone, but especially wheelchair users and guide dog users, to correctly position themselves to approach and enter the building.

- The lighting levels on entry into a building should be graduated to allow adjustment from a bright exterior to a lower internal light level.

## Entrance doors

Doors should allow easy entry and egress. Factors to be taken into account include the minimum clear opening width of the door, the resistance that needs to be overcome to open the door, the opening mechanism and the provision of vision panels.

- Entrance doors should give a minimum clear opening width of 800 mm through one leaf. The opening width should be increased to accommodate any projections such as full-height pulls or a weatherboard.

Where there are double doors, at least one leaf should be of sufficient width to allow entry (800 mm minimum or greater if required), as people may not be able to open both leaves simultaneously.

- Single doors should have at least 300 mm space beside the leading edge of the door to allow anyone with limited mobility to approach and open the door.
- Door closers should be avoided if possible, but where necessary should be adjusted to the minimum force necessary, be slow in operation and regularly maintained. The opening force at the leading edge of the door should not exceed 30 N from 0° to 30° and not exceed 22.5 N from 30° to 60° of the opening cycle. Delayed action closers are preferred and should be fitted where possible.
- Outward opening doors should be recessed or the swing area adequately protected to prevent collisions.
- Vision panels should be provided in doors in frequent use. The minimum zone of visibility should be between 500 mm and 1500 mm above the floor.

- Glazed doors and side panels may require manifestation to increase visibility. Manifestation should be well contrasted against its background and highly visible at all times of day, and where appropriate, in both natural and artificial light.

> The provision of good, clear manifestation at design stage will remove the possibility of *ad hoc* and possibly unattractive additions later on.
>
> The design of manifestation can offer an excellent opportunity to promote the company or service at the very place most people will be looking when they enter a building or move around it.

- Where glass doors are part of a glazed screen there should be a contrasting frame or other means of differentiating doors and screen.
- Edges of glazed doors should be clearly visible when the doors are in an open position.
- Door furniture should be distinguishable, in terms of visual contrast, from the door and be positioned where it can be easily reached, gripped and used with minimum effort.

> Full-height door handles and other features, such as weatherboards, must not restrict the clear opening width of doors.

- Lever-style handles allow use by elbows or the edge of the hand. A return at the end will prevent the hand from slipping off the handle and help prevent clothing being caught.
- A kicking plate can protect a door from damage caused by wheelchair footrests if full width and at least 400 mm deep.

**Figure 4.21** A platform lift added beside a stepped change of level at the entrance of a historic building can improve access.

## Automatic doors

Automatic doors provide good, easy access and will benefit all building users. Sliding doors are preferable in areas of heavy traffic. Where swing doors are used, care should be taken to protect the door swing area. Advice on the presence and operating style of automatic doors should be provided on approach, using signs; a change in floor surface can also be used.

- Activation can be automatic or manual. Where there are manual activators, they should be clearly signed, identifiable (perhaps by the use of good visual contrast) and positioned and designed to allow easy approach and use.
- Swing doors require protection to swing area, particularly if opening towards users or into a circulation area.
- All automatic doors require safety devices to ensure that the door does not close if there is an obstruction. With the exception of doors fitted with low-energy systems, a photocell

**Figure 4.22** Where there is a choice of doors, the majority of people prefer to use the automatic door.

method should be used to ensure closing does not begin until the doorway is clear.

- Low energy swing door operators do not require additional safety equipment such as presence sensors if they have low opening forces, low opening speed and obstacle default function to ensure the door stops immediately if it touches an obstacle.
- Sliding doors generally provide very good access and may be preferred in areas of heavy traffic.
- Doors should remain open for long enough to allow a slow moving person to pass through.

Automatic doors generally offer very good access for disabled people, but doors that swing towards the user can be dangerous and off-putting. Tactile information could be provided by the use of a different floor surface in front of the door to warn of the direction of the door swing.

**Figure 4.23** Automatic swing doors should be clearly signed and the swing area protected.

- Sliding/folding doors are useful where space is restricted and often can be used in existing door openings.

## Revolving doors

Revolving doors do not provide good access for everyone. Even the larger automatic revolving doors, sometimes found at shopping centres or supermarkets, are not recommended as many people find them difficult or uncomfortable to use. Wheelchair users, people using mobility aids such as sticks or crutches, guide dog users and older people may not be able, or may not have the confidence, to use any size or type of revolving door.

A revolving door at the entrance to a building will not give a message of accessibility and openness, and, importantly, it will cause visitors to be segregated on entry to the building.

Where they are used, there must be an alternative entrance with a clear opening width of at least 800 mm, immediately adjacent and clearly visible. This should be a swing door, preferably automated and always operational.

Where swing doors are provided as an alternative entrance, they should be operational at all times when the building is open and the revolving door is in use. If the alternative entrance is kept locked, the message given to visitors is 'you can come in if you can use the revolving door, otherwise you will have to wait for someone to come and let you in'. Many people will see this arrangement as discriminatory.

Where climate control is a concern, two sets of automatic sliding doors can be used, offset, with a lobby between.

## Thresholds

Thresholds should be flush wherever possible. Opening a door whilst simultaneously negotiating a raised threshold can be extremely difficult for some users and any change in level can present a tripping hazard.

There need not be a conflict between user needs and water-proofing, with careful design and management both sets of needs can be met.

- Thresholds should be flush wherever possible.
- Where a raised threshold is unavoidable, the maximum change in level should be 15 mm, providing the raised section is clearly visible and the floor finish graded to provide a flush finish. However, some ambulant disabled people will find any changes in level difficult, if not impossible, to negotiate.

## Doormats

Inside entrances a floor surface should be provided that will remove rainwater from shoes and wheels to prevent floor finishes becoming slippery. Where a doormat is provided, it should be firm and flush to allow easy wheeled passage.

- Coir and other deep pile materials are not suitable for wheeled passage.
- Mats that are not properly recessed can cause tripping.

**Figure 4.24** Good use of fixed mats – but loose mats represent a serious tripping hazard.

> Any fitted doormats should be flush with the floor, firm and close fitting to the mat well.

## Lobbies

Lobbies should be of sufficient size to allow easy access, egress and manoeuvre. The layout and the door design should allow all users, including wheelchair users, ambulant disabled people, guide dog users and people with children or pushchairs, to open doors independently and move clear of one door before negotiating a second.

## Entry systems

All entry systems should be designed and located to allow easy approach and use. Security systems should suit the requirements of all people entering a building, including wheelchair users. Turnstiles or barriers that segregate people on entry to a building should not be used.

- Entry systems should be suitable to meet the needs of all users, including those with limited dexterity, visual and speech impairments and those users who are deaf or hard of hearing.

- Entry phones should be clearly identifiable (perhaps with the use of visual contrast) and should be placed at a height that can be operated from a standing or seated position. The maximum height of the highest operating button should not be more than 1200 mm above finished floor level.
- The design of press keypads should be suitable to allow operation by people with restricted dexterity and incorporate sufficient contrast to be seen. They should also be set at a height that can be used from either a standing or seated position.
- If a control device contains an audible communication system, perhaps to announce arrival or to seek assistance, the needs of people who are deaf or hard of hearing must be considered, perhaps by incorporating an inductive coupler and an LED display.

**Figure 4.25** Systems used to control access and for communication must be accessible, and usable, for everyone.

- Clear, unambiguous information on what disabled people should do to attract attention or summon assistance, if required, should be displayed on or near the control device. Any contact phone numbers that could be used by mobile phone users to call assistance should be clearly displayed on or adjacent to the entry control device.
- Management responses to dealing with someone who requires assistance to enter a building or other environment should be written down and practised to ensure they are operable at all times. Staff should also be fully trained in dealing with the communication needs of people who are deaf or hard of hearing.

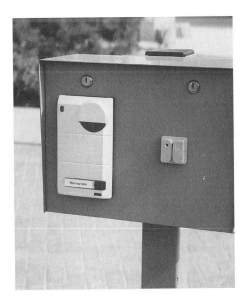

**Figure 4.26** This car park control requires reach, dexterity, speech, hearing, and a right arm. It is possible to hold a driver's licence without one or more of the above but you need all of them if you wish to enter this car park. Is this reasonable provision?

If an entry system is being used to control entry to a building in which an employment opportunity or service is being provided, there may be a duty under the DDA not to discriminate in allowing access to the building. It may be possible to replace an unsatisfactory system with an alternative – perhaps one incorporating CCTV – or to use appropriate management techniques and staff training until the system can be replaced, but the issue cannot be ignored.

## Exits

Exit doors, particularly those used for emergency egress, should incorporate the features recommended for entrances as appropriate.

## Reception areas

On entering a building the location of the reception point should be obvious and logically placed. Reception areas should be well lit, routes should be clearly defined and unobstructed, and there should be clear information on facilities available within the building.

- The waiting area should be quiet and well lit to allow easier communication, especially for people with hearing impairments.
- There should be clear unobstructed routes with sufficient space for manoeuvring.
- All furniture should have adequate visual contrast with the background against which it will be viewed. In smaller areas, this may simply be the walls, in larger areas it may be the wall, floor or other furniture.
- If there is an audible communication system, it should be supplemented by visual information.
- Where there is likely to be a high level of background noise, an induction loop should be provided and its presence indicated by the standard symbol (see also *Reception desks*).

**Plate 1** Contrast between floors, walls and features can help people navigate around a building.

**Plate 2** Reception desks should be clearly visible. A low section with an overhang allows close approach by wheelchair users.

**Plate 3** Visual contrast can help identify critical surfaces and special features – but light reflectance values should be checked to ensure adequate contrast.

**Plate 4** Doors should contrast with their surroundings and door furniture should contrast with the door.

**Plate 5** Manifestation should be able to be clearly seen in all lighting conditions. It can also be used to help identify entrances.

**Plate 6** Fittings in toilets should contrast with their background; a different coloured floor would help with orientation.

**Plate 7** The projecting section of this sign indicates facilities on this floor of the building. Information in Braille is located on the horizontal surface.

**Plate 8** Good use of colour and contrast – the signboard contrasts with its background and the information contrasts with the signboard.

Fully trained staff at key points, such as car park entrances, reception and help desks, can improve considerably the perceived and actual accesssibility of a building or facility whilst also addressing many security and safety issues.

Staff should be trained in understanding the needs of disabled people and how to interact with them. They should know of any potential dangers or hazards that may affect disabled people using the environment and be aware of how to help if required. They should know routes to and locations of all important facilities, such as accessible toilets. Key staff should also understand the needs of people with visual impairments and undergo basic mobility training to allow them to assist people if required. They should also have some basic training in clear speaking and perhaps basic sign language, to assist people who are deaf or hard of hearing.

Seating should be made available where there is a likelihood of waiting being necessary. To ensure that the needs of as many users as possible are met, a selection of seating should be provided, with different seat heights and with and without arms. If fixed seating is provided, there should be some movable seating to accommodate wheelchair users sitting with other people.

- Where seating is arranged in rows, there should be clear space of 900 mm minimum width (1200 mm preferred) in front of a row of seats to allow people to pass along a row to a seating position.
- A mixture of fixed and removable seats should be provided to accommodate different seating layouts and numbers of disabled people.
- Integrated space for wheelchairs should be provided to allow wheelchair users to sit alongside seated companions.
- Space adjacent to seating should be provided for working dogs.
- Seats should be of sufficient size to accommodate larger people and some should have firm seats and armrests that are sturdy enough to assist users when sitting or standing.

## Reception desks

The reception desk should be easily seen and appropriately signed. There should be sufficient manoeuvring space to allow people to approach and use the desk. Communication at the desk should be possible at seated and standing heights (see Plates 1 and 2 in the colour plate section).

---

The design of a reception desk, and particularly the requirement for a low section for the benefit of wheelchair users, is dependent upon the way in which the desk will be used. If no paperwork needs to be completed at the desk, a lowered section may be desirable, but is not essential provided communication is possible when seated. However, if people visiting the building are required to sign in, or fill in other paperwork, then some means of doing this must be provided.

Where there is a lowered section, there should also be a knee recess to allow a wheelchair user to pull up close enough to use the desk. It may be possible to alter an existing desk or to add a drop-down shelf that could be lowered when required.

In existing buildings, looking at the way a desk is actually used can allow a decision to be made on whether immediate replacement or alteration is necessary, or whether this can wait until the desk is due to be replaced or refurbished.

---

- Access for wheelchair users should be possible to both staff and visitor sides of reception desks and counters.
- A low height counter or lowered section should be provided where it is necessary for communication or signing in. Seating should be provided at low height counters.
- The receptionist's face should be clearly visible and well lit to allow lip reading. If there is a glazed screen, it should be able to be opened to allow for direct communication. If it cannot be opened, or if there is likely to be background noise, an induction loop should be provided for the benefit of hearing aid users.

Glass partitions should be avoided because they make lip reading difficult for deaf or hard of hearing users. If glass partitions are unavoidable, non-reflective glazing and a speech enhancing system should be used.

- Induction loops are often fitted at reception desks and can be used by people with a hearing aid equipped with a T switch. This is estimated to be about 1.5 million of the 8.5 million people in the UK who have a hearing impairment or loss. For the others, good communication by key staff and other methods of assisting people who are deaf or hard of hearing must be considered. Good lighting design, appropriate decoration to surfaces, staff speaking clearly, information being available in alternative formats (for example, 14 point sans serif font on non-reflective yellow paper) and, if possible, some awareness or training of British Sign Language are all important.

**Figure 4.27**  This desk has a low section – but the writing shelf and the lack of knee space would prevent easy use by a wheelchair user.

> The provision of an induction loop alone does not mean that an employer or service provider has met the needs of the deaf and hard of hearing population.

# Horizontal circulation

## Ease of navigation

A rational and simple building layout is easier to navigate and remember.

The entrance to a building should be located clearly and in an obvious position. The reception area should be close to the entrance and give easy access to circulation routes throughout the building. Circulation areas should be clear of hazards and use colour and contrast to identify routes, layouts and obstacles.

Clear directional information should be provided with resting places on longer routes and conveniently located and clearly signed lifts where required. A simple, well-planned circulation layout will encourage easy orientation.

Circulation routes through open-plan spaces should have sufficient clear width, which should be maintained when layouts are altered. It can be helpful to define routes using visual or textural contrast.

## Corridors and passageways

Corridor widths should accommodate wheelchair manoeuvre and passing, guide dog use and, where relevant, the needs of people with pushchairs.

- A minimum width of 1200 mm is recommended for corridors and other circulation routes. This width is essential at door-opening positions to allow a wheelchair user to turn through 90°. Wider corridors will be required where there is heavy use.
- In buildings where there are likely to be significant numbers of wheelchair users the corridors should be at least 1800 mm wide, or have passing places at reasonable intervals.

**Figure 4.28** Route to the reception desk is identified; however, visual contrast would have made this information available to a greater number of people.

- Where corridor width is restricted, for example in existing buildings, wider door openings should be considered and passing places provided.
- Corridor widths should be unobstructed, with wall-mounted fittings recessed wherever possible.
- Outward opening doors can be hazardous, particularly to people with sight impairments, and should be recessed.
- Splayed or rounded corners can ease circulation along corridors.

## Surfaces

The choice of floor and wall surfaces can greatly affect the ease of use of an environment. Hard surfaces can cause sound reverberation and high levels of background noise, which can cause difficulties in communication. Thick pile carpets will hinder wheelchair passage. Shiny floors can appear slippery and are not

**Figure 4.29** How many doors are there? Reflective finishes can be very confusing for someone with poor vision.

**Figure 4.30** Many people would find this floor finish disconcerting, but especially those with poor vision, older people and people using mobility aids such as crutches. It may not be the selection of the floor covering that is the problem, but the way it is being cleaned and the impact of daylight and artificial lighting.

liked by visually impaired and older people who feel unsafe when walking on them. Heavily patterned floor finishes can be confusing to people with visual impairments. Adequate visual contrast is essential to define surfaces and objects placed upon them (see Plate 3 in the colour plate section).

- Highly reflective finishes should be avoided for floor, walls, doors and ceilings.
- Visual contrast will help define floor, wall, ceiling and door surfaces and objects placed upon them.
- Floor surfaces should be firm and flush.
- Floors should be slip resistant, but also not look as if they might be slippery.
- Junctions between different floor finishes should be detailed to prevent tripping and allow easy wheeled passage.
- Where carpet is laid, it should be firmly fixed, non-directional and have a shallow dense pile.
- Surface-laid rugs or mats must be avoided in public buildings, as they present tripping or slipping hazards.
- The choice of materials for floor, wall and ceiling surfaces should give an acoustic environment that allows audible information to be heard and aids orientation.
- Textured surfaces can be used to impart information to people with visual impairments. It is important to use recognised textures or to provide a key.

## Glazed walls and screens

- Glazed walls and screens that are adjacent to doors, or form part of an enclosure, should have clear manifestation, each element at least 150 mm square, which contrasts with the background in all lighting conditions. The manifestation should be placed at standing and seated eye level, 1500 mm and 1050 mm above floor level.

## Handrails

Many older people and people with visual impairments will benefit from the provision of handrails along corridors to assist with physical support or give tactile information.

**Figure 4.31**  Are the squares manifestation on the glass or decoration on the train? Critical information is lost – even for those with good vision.

- Where handrails are provided, they should be designed to be gripped, be well contrasted with the supporting wall and be as continuous as possible.

  For detailed guidance on handrail design see *Internal steps and stairs.*

## Internal doors

Doors on circulation routes will be less of a barrier if they are light enough to open easily, give the required clear width through one leaf and have handles that can be used with minimum effort.

### Door width and location

- Internal doors should have a minimum clear opening width of 800 mm.

- The minimum opening width must take into account any door furniture and doorstops.

> The layout of furniture and fittings, in a building in use, may affect the clear opening width of a door.

- Double doors should provide the minimum required opening width through one leaf.

> Where overall width is restricted, double doors can have leaves of unequal size to give the necessary clear opening width through one leaf.

- There should be sufficient space around doors to allow users to manoeuvre and approach. A minimum space of 300 mm should be provided adjacent to the leading edge of a door that swings towards the user to allow easy independent use.
- Doors opening into a circulation route should be recessed or have the swing area protected.

## Door furniture

- Door furniture should be visually distinguishable from the door and be designed and positioned to be easily reached, gripped and used with minimum effort.
- Lever-style handles allow use by elbows or the edge of the hand. A return at the end will prevent the hand from slipping off the handle and helps prevent clothing being caught.
- A kicking plate can protect a door from damage caused by wheelchair footrests if full width and at least 400 mm deep.

**Figure 4.32** A good style of door handle is essential to many disabled people.

The use of appropriately contrasted door handles, fingerplates, hinges and kicking plates can assist people with visual impairments to recognise the presence of a door, even if the door is the same colour as the wall surrounding it. There are very few things in the built environment that mimic the visual appearance of the pattern of door furniture. The colour and shape of door furniture can be indicators not only of the presence of a door, but also of the way it opens.

This type of information, often giving a person with a visual impairment hints about things they may well have once seen in more detail, can help enormously when someone is moving through a building and searching for features. Similarly, the careful use of subtle shadows, such as those around the panels on a panelled door, can give very useful clues to the presence of a door, even if there is little colour contrast between the door and its surround.

Eighty-two per cent of people with impaired vision actually see something; their ability to use that residual vision to gather information about their environment can be maximised by careful design.

Kicking plates should either be glued to the door or fixed
with countersunk screws. Projecting screw heads may cause
injury to a disabled person and/or damage to the wheelchair.

**Door closers**    Door closers should be adjusted to the
minimum force necessary, be slow in operation and regularly
maintained.

- Guidance recommends that the opening force at the leading
  edge of the door should not exceed 30 N from 0° to 30° and
  not exceed 22.5 N from 30° to 60° of the opening cycle.
- Delayed action closers are preferred and should be fitted
  wherever possible.
- Where a door has no closing device it is useful to fit a pull
  handle to help people close the door behind them.

Revisions to the guidance given in AD M on door opening forces
have been made since the publication of the 2004 edition and are
listed on the website www.communities.gov.uk under Building
Regulations, in the Approved Document M Frequently Asked
Questions (FAQ) pages.

**Fire doors**    Fire doors fitted with self-closing devices can
prevent easy circulation around a building. It is important that
doors and closers are specified that will allow easy use, while
maintaining the required level of fire protection.

- Where the force required to open a fire-resisting door on a
  circulation route exceeds that described above, an electrically
  powered hold-open device, conforming to the requirements of
  BS EN 1155, should be installed. Door closing can be activated
  by a signal from the fire alarm system, manually or by fail safety
  operation.
- If smoke seals are required, installing an angle seal as an
  independent item in the doorframe can reduce the force
  required to open the door.

Even when a door is held open, the force required to open it from a closed position should still be checked when carrying out an audit. When the hold-open device is deactivated in an emergency, it is essential to ensure that the door can be opened easily to allow people to escape or that there is a management procedure in place to deal with such an eventuality. What must be avoided is the possibility of the door trapping people when an emergency occurs.

## Visibility

- Visual contrast will allow doors and/or doorframes to be distinguished from their surroundings (see Plate 4 in the colour plate section).
- Glazed doors and side panels should be clearly defined with manifestation, at least 150 mm square, at 1050 mm and 1500 mm above the floor to increase visibility. Manifestation should be well contrasted against its background and highly visible at all times of day and in all lighting conditions (see Plate 5 in the colour plate section).
- Fully glazed doors that form part of a glass screen should be clearly differentiated from the screen.

Sometimes, designers and building managers are unsure whether it is necessary to contrast the door with the surrounding wall or if simply contrasting the architrave with the wall, and having the door the same colour as the wall, is adequate.

Most visually impaired people have a strong preference for the whole door being contrasted with the surrounding wall. Contrasting only the architrave will still make most people aware of the possible presence of a door, but it will take longer for them to be sure they are seeing a door as opposed to some other feature.

**Figure 4.33** Is the manifestation adequately contrasted against its background at all times?

**Vision panels**    Doors on circulation routes should have vision panels. These are also useful on other doors to allow people to determine whether a room is in use.

- Vision panels should provide a minimum zone of visibility of 500 mm to 1500 mm above floor level.

**Automatic opening**    Automatic or power-assisted opening devices will be of benefit to many users and some can be fitted to existing doors. Activation can be automatic or manual. Where there are manual activators they should be clearly signed, positioned and designed to allow easy approach and use (see also *Entrance doors*).

Vision panels can be useful for people who are deaf or hard of hearing to help them gain the sort of information that others might gather audibly. For example, if someone knocks on a door seeking entry into a room, they may be unable to hear a response of 'come in' or 'please wait'. The only way that they will know if their knock has been heard, or indeed if the room is occupied, will be to open the door and look, which may not be appropriate. Vision panels can help to prevent this problem.

Vision panels can also save time when checking evacuation from a building in an emergency – good building management and accessibility working hand in hand.

**Lobbies**    Internal lobbies should be avoided wherever possible. If unavoidable, they should be of sufficient size to allow easy access, egress and manoeuvre. The layout and door design should allow all users, including wheelchair users, ambulant disabled people, guide dog users and people with children or pushchairs, to open doors independently and move clear of one door before negotiating a second.

## Vertical circulation

Stairs, steps, ramps and lifts all provide means of vertical movement within a building. All should be designed to allow easy and safe use.

- Ramps and/or lifts should be provided at all changes of level for people who cannot, or prefer not to, use stairs.
- All internal changes of level, including single steps and short ramps, should be clearly indicated to reduce the risk of tripping or losing balance.

## Internal steps and stairs

Stairs are the most common means of achieving change of level and should be designed to accommodate safe and easy use by everyone. Lack of suitable handrails for support, projecting nosings or open risers that can trap toes, and lack of warning on approach can result in stairs that are difficult for people to use and potentially hazardous.

- Handrails should always be provided, however short the flight.
- Isolated single steps should be avoided where possible.
- The unobstructed width of stairs should be at least 1200 mm.
- A level landing of at least 1200 mm should be provided at the top and bottom of each flight of stairs.
- The maximum rise between landings should be no more than 12 risers. (In small premises a maximum of 16 risers may be acceptable.)

## Risers and goings

- The height of the riser should be between 150 mm and 170 mm. The going should be 250 mm to 300 mm, with a preference for 300 mm.
- Open risers and deeply recessed risers should not be used as they can catch toes, sticks, callipers, etc. Open risers can also be visually confusing for people with sight impairments.
- The nosing of each step in a flight of stairs should be adequately contrasted with the remainder of the step and the floor covering adjacent to the top and bottom of the flight. Guidance given in Approved Document M states that all nosings should be made apparent by means of a permanently contrasting material 55 mm wide on both the tread and the riser. Patterned highlighting, especially 'sharks tooth', should not be used as it can give a confusing message, which can be potentially dangerous.
- Steps without projecting nosings are preferred. If there is an overlap it should be less than 25 mm.
- Tapered treads and spiral stairs are not recommended for use in public buildings.

**Figure 4.34** Open risers should always be avoided; they can be visually confusing and catch toes, sticks, callipers, etc.

**Figure 4.35** Each step nosing should contrast visually with the remainder of the tread and should be clearly visible when ascending and descending stairs.

Steps with goings that are less than the recommended minimum length can be difficult or impossible for some people to use. If someone is unable to place his or her whole foot on the step, all the weight will be supported on the sole of the foot when ascending the steps and on the heel when descending, the only alternative being to turn the foot sideways to obtain the maximum area of support.

All these manoeuvres would be extremely difficult for many disabled and older people to perform and this may result in them not being able to use the stairs. There may also be consequences relating to the DDA where a physical feature makes it impossible or unreasonably difficult for disabled people to access a service or employment opportunity.

**Figure 4.36** The area below overhanging stairs should be guarded.

The design of a stair should not present a danger to users of a building, either when using it or moving past it. Importantly, the underside of staircases should be protected to prevent all users, but especially those with a visual impairment, colliding with the structure of the stair.

Under-stair areas with low headroom should be protected with a fixed rail or houseplants to avoid the possibility of all users, but especially those with a visual impairment, from colliding with the staircase.

**Handrails**    Handrails are used for a variety of reasons when ascending or descending a stair, and the design and provision of them should take varying needs of users into account wherever possible. For example, people with impaired vision often rely heavily on handrails to orientate themselves on staircases, to determine when they have reached the top or bottom of a flight of stairs or steps or in establishing a change of direction. All people will need a handrail that is easy to grip if they trip or fall on the stairs. Therefore, it is important that a handrail is visible, reachable, is strong enough to provide physical support if needed and offers good tactile information about the stair to the user, both when ascending and descending the stairs.

Except in existing buildings, where narrow staircases and other safety issues may prevent it, handrails should always be provided to each side of a flight of steps. People may be weaker on one side and require a handrail for support. (It should be noted that the installation of a platform or stair lift might prevent the use of one handrail.) The division of wider flights into separate channels will allow easier access to handrails when many people are using the stair.

The horizontal extension of a handrail beyond the first and last steps allows an individual to steady or to brace him- or herself before ascending or descending, provides support to ascend the final riser and will signal the start or finish of the flight to people with visual impairments.

- A handrail, properly visually contrasted against its background, should always be provided to both sides, however short the flight.
- Handrails must be of a size and shape that is easy to grip and of circular or oval profile. A circular handrail should have a diameter between 40 mm and 50 mm and the preferred dimensions for a handrail with an oval profile are 50 mm wide and 38 mm deep. The oval profile should have rounded edges with a radius of at least 15 mm.

A non-circular handrail with a flat upper surface gives better hand and forearm support. However, it must be able to be gripped.

- When fixed to, or placed adjacent to a wall, a clear space of at least 60 mm should be provided between the handrail and the wall surface. To minimise the risk of supports to the handrail injuring a user's hand or reducing the ability to grip the rail, a clearance of at least 50 mm should be provided between the handrail and any cranked support or balustrade.
- Handrails should be continuous to stairs and landings, be able to be gripped along their full length and extend horizontally at least 300 mm beyond the first and last nosing in the flight.
- The vertical height to the top of a handrail should be between 900 mm and 1000 mm from the pitch line of a flight of steps, and between 900 mm and 1100 mm from the surface of a landing.
- A central handrail should be provided on wide flights.
- The handrail should either return to the wall or have a positive end.
- Nylon and timber handrails are pleasant to the touch and are best suited for people who may be affected by the contact temperature of a handrail. Steel handrails will tend to be cold to the touch.

**Figure 4.37** Contrasting nosings and well-designed handrails can help people use stairs.

Tactile warning studs or markers on the handrail can be a very useful indicator of the beginning or end of flight and to indicate the floor level reached.

**Hazard warning**    There can be a risk of tripping or losing balance particularly at the head of a flight of steps and so a warning surface is recommended to alert people to the change of level.

- A tactile warning surface (corduroy pattern) can be provided at the top and bottom of each flight. The surface should extend beyond the width of the flight if practicable. If the warning surface is not used there should be a change of colour and texture in the floor finish on approach to the stair.
- Where there is access beneath a stair, the underside should be protected to prevent people from colliding with the structure.

**Figure 4.38** Tactile hazard warning can alert people to the presence of a stair.

> Care should be taken to ensure that stairs are not a continuation of the normal line of pedestrian travel, for example along a corridor, without any warning given of their presence.

## Internal ramps

Ramps should be used where it is necessary to address unavoidable changes in level and not simply to overcome changes of level that could have been avoided by good, thoughtful design. The presence of a ramp should be clearly indicated to warn people of its presence and prevent tripping. Visual contrast in floor finish can be used.

Some people may have difficulty walking on a sloping surface and will prefer to use steps rather than a ramp. Wherever ramps are provided steps should accompany them.

- Ramps in internal corridors should be highlighted to increase visibility.
- Ramps should always have suitably designed handrails.

With the exception of those issues relating specifically to the external environment, the design considerations for internal ramps are as those for external ramped access (see *External ramps*).

## Lighting on stairs and ramps

Good lighting is essential on stairs and ramps, though bright directional lighting, glare or strong shadows can be disorientating and cause accidents.

- Illuminance at tread/floor level should be at least 200 lux.
- Lighting incorporated into stair risers is likely to be disorientating to all users and should not be used.

> Carefully positioned lighting can be used to help identify the location of risers and goings in stairs. Contrasting nosings are always recommended to identify steps, but if they are not present and cannot be added, for example in some historic properties, good lighting can help.

## Escalators

Escalators can be useful where there is a need to move large numbers of people between floors, but can present a barrier to many people. They should be carefully designed to allow safe use and there should always be an alternative means of access provided for wheelchair users, people with pushchairs, guide dog users or any other people who do not wish to use the escalator.

- The entry and exit to the escalator should be clearly visible, well lit and free from unnecessary obstructions.
- There is no requirement in regulations to provide a tactile floor surface on the approach to an escalator. However, it is useful to

provide some contrast in the floor covering at the top and bottom landing to alert people to the presence of an escalator.

- The direction of travel should be clearly indicated, possibly by a red or green light. This is of particular importance where escalator direction is altered, for example during busy periods. The indicator should be located and designed to be clearly visible on approach to the escalator.
- Audible announcements can be used to warn of approaching end of escalator.
- Handrails should have visual contrast and extend at least 150 mm beyond the entry and exit points.
- Handrails should move at the same speed as the steps.
- Side panels should be non-reflective. Back illuminated panels can be visually confusing.
- Contrasting nosings should be visible when both ascending and descending.
- Stationary escalators used as stairs will present difficulties for many people due to the varying and deep height of the risers.
- Lifts should be located near to escalators and clearly signed from the escalator.

---

Guide dog users are often prevented from using escalators, not because of their visual impairment, but because of the need to carry their guide dogs when travelling on the escalator. This can be a difficult task for many guide dog users, and impossible for some.

---

## Passenger conveyors (travelators)

Some people will be unable or unwilling to use passenger conveyors and an alternative from of access should always be provided.

Design requirements for passenger conveyors will be similar to those for escalators. It is critical to provide warning of the end of the journey.

**Figure 4.39** Where a travelator is inclined the gradient should be low to allow easy and safe access.

- There should be good visual contrast between the moving surface and the fixed floor and good lighting in this area.
- Audible announcement and visual clues should be used to give warning of start and end of moving surface.
- There should be handrails and guarding along each side of the conveyor.
- If inclined, the gradient should be low. Steep gradients can be difficult to use when stationary and cause wheelchairs to tip up.

## Platform lifts and stair lifts

Platform lifts and wheelchair stair lifts can be used to overcome changes of level where it is not possible to use a ramp or passenger lift. Stair lifts with a seat, without a wheelchair platform, are generally used in private dwellings, although they may be provided for disabled employees in the workplace.

**Figure 4.40** When a vertical platform lift is provided it should be adjacent to the stair with which it is associated.

> If a stair lift is installed, there will often be a resulting loss of a handrail to the stair. This can be difficult, especially in housing, where providing such facilities to meet the needs of one user may impinge upon the ability of another person in the house to use the stairs safely.

**Platform lifts**   Platform lifts have a guarded platform that travels vertically. They are used mainly to travel short distances and should be easy and safe to use by an unaccompanied wheelchair user. Platform lifts should conform to BS 6440.

- Ideally lifts should be located adjacent to the stair with which they are associated.
- Approaches to the lift should be kept clear at all times.
- Clear concise instructions on lift use should be provided, including how to summon help if required.

**Figure 4.41** A vertical platform lift can be added to an existing building to help provide equal access to services.

- Lifts should be fitted with an alarm in case users get into difficulty.
- Maximum rise is 2 m in public buildings without a lift enclosure or floor penetration, or up to 4 m in private dwellings or in public buildings where there is a lift enclosure.
- Minimum clear dimensions of the platform should be 1050 mm wide and 1250 mm long.

**Wheelchair stair lifts**   Wheelchair stair lifts travel up the pitch line of a stair. Their use is not recommended in new buildings, though they may be useful in providing access in existing buildings where it is not possible to fit a passenger lift or a platform lift. Wheelchair stair lifts should conform to BS 5776 and in particular BS 5776:1996, Annex A. Prior to the installation of a stair lift in a public building, the Building Control Authority and the Fire Authority should be consulted and means of escape requirements met.

Assistance is usually required to use the lift and access to the stair will be limited while the lift is in use.

Wheelchair stair lifts can be installed to straight and curved flights and can continue across landings. Approach to the platform can be straight or lateral. Lateral approach will require a wider platform.

- In parked position the stair lift should not obstruct the required clear width of the stair.
- When installed in new buildings, there should be a minimum clear width of 600 mm between the folded down platform of a wheelchair stair lift and the handrail opposite.
- A means of summoning assistance should be provided. Stair lifts in public buildings should be fitted with an alarm that conforms to the requirements of ISO 9386-2.
- A fold-down seat is useful for ambulant disabled users.

## Passenger lifts

The provision of suitable, user-friendly lifts will have a major impact on the accessibility of a building. Lifts are an essential amenity for many people and can provide good, easy access for everyone.

> Visual and tactile information should be used to identify the location of a lift. However, signs in and around the lift should be kept to a minimum to allow essential signs to be prominent.

The location, size and number of lifts should suit the building type and anticipated traffic. Wherever possible, there should be a minimum of two passenger lifts available for use in public buildings, to allow for one lift being out of action due to maintenance or break-down. Where only one lift is provided for public use, consideration should be given to making available a staff lift as a temporary alternative.

- All lifts should be safe and easy to use and their location should be clearly marked.

- There should be adequate manoeuvring space outside the lift to allow wheelchair users to turn to reverse into the lift car, or to turn, having reversed out. A clear space of at least 1500 mm by 1500 mm is recommended.
- A lift car 1100 mm wide by 1400 mm deep will accommodate one wheelchair user and one accompanying person. There will be insufficient space to allow the wheelchair user to turn conveniently. A wheelchair user entering forwards will need to reverse out and this should be taken into account in landing design.

The current minimum recommended lift car dimensions are 1100 mm by 1400 mm. If the lift car is smaller than this, it may still be suitable for a wheelchair user who is able to operate the control buttons without assistance. If the lift cannot be used, working practices could be altered in the short term, for example, a wheelchair user could work on the ground floor of the building instead of one of the upper floors. In the longer term, a new lift should be installed with the appropriate dimensions.

- A lift car 2000 mm wide by 1400 mm deep will accommodate any type of wheelchair, together with several other passengers. There is sufficient space for wheelchair users and people with walking aids to turn through 180°.

Where a lift is used for access between two floors only the provision of doors at opposite ends will allow wheelchair users to enter and leave more easily.

Lift cars must meet the floor level to provide level access and egress into and out of the lift. Uneven levels can be a potential hazard, particularly for visually impaired users, ambulant disabled people and wheelchair users.

   The lift machinery should be checked and adjusted if necessary as part of a programmed maintenance policy.

## Doors

- Lift doors should be clearly distinguishable from their surroundings using visual contrast.
- Doors should give a minimum of 800 mm clear opening width (820 mm preferred).

In certain situations where wider wheelchairs are commonly used, for example, sports wheelchairs in a sports centre, a wider lift door may be needed.

- Door control should be by photocell to ensure closing does not begin until doorway is clear. Audible warning devices announcing door opening and closing should be provided.
- Lifts should have a dwell time at landings of 5 seconds after doors have opened.

The doors to the lift often present the greatest hazard to the disabled user. The minimum dwell time to allow a person to enter the lift before the doors begin to close should be 5 seconds. A dwell time of less than 5 seconds can cause people to feel anxious and worry about being caught in a closing door.

## Controls and indicators

- Call and control buttons should be located between 900 mm and 1100 mm from the floor, and at least 400 mm from any return wall. Buttons should be of sufficient size, 20 mm to 30 mm diameter, for easy identification and activation, have visual contrast with their background and have symbols in relief (between 1 mm and 1.5 mm) to enable tactile reading.
- The lift control buttons should not be touch sensitive.
- There should be audible and visual indication of button activation, lift arrival and direction of travel. Inside the lift

**Figure 4.42** Lift buttons located horizontally can be easier to reach.

there should also be audible and visual indication of floor level reached.

- Floor level indicators should be positioned so that they can be seen when the lift is full.
- Lift control panels should be located on both side walls of lift car, within reach of a wheelchair user who is facing the rear wall of the lift.
- Vertical strips of lighting on either side of the control panel creates glare and should be avoided.
- If there is a bank of lifts, there should be clear indication of lift arriving and time for all users to approach and enter the lift.
- A sign indicating the floor level should be provided on each lift landing on the wall opposite the lift.
- Buttons essential for lift operation should be positioned separately from those rarely used.
- Alarms should have tactile information and adequate visual contrast. Alarms should have visual and audible indication to acknowledge request for assistance.
- Any emergency system that relies upon audible communication should be supported with text information, such as a textphone or written information explaining emergency procedures.

- Emergency telephones should be fitted with inductive couplers to allow use by hearing aid users.

## Fittings

- A support rail, 35–50 mm diameter, located 900 mm above floor level, should be provided to the rear and side walls to assist navigation for visually impaired people and as a physical support for older people or those who experience difficulties with balance.
- A mirror fitted to the rear wall, above handrail level, will help wheelchair users who have to reverse out and will allow reading of floor level indicators located above the lift doors. A mirror covering the whole wall should not be used, as it may be confusing for people with visual impairments.
- The floor surface should be firm to allow easy wheelchair manoeuvre and slip resistant.

> Slip-resistant floor surfaces in lifts are of particular benefit to people who use walking aids such as sticks or crutches, and older people.

- Visually and acoustically reflective wall surfaces should be avoided as they can cause problems for people with sensory impairments.
- Fold-down seats could be provided in larger lifts.
- Lighting within the lift car should be a minimum of 100 lux (200 lux preferred). Lighting should be even and free of glare.

> Where it is impossible to provide lift access in an existing building it may be necessary to relocate or duplicate essential services and facilities to ensure that everyone can access them.

**Evacuation lifts**    Passenger lifts that are to be used for emergency evacuation should have an independent power supply and conform to the relevant recommendations of BS 5588.

# Facilities

## Toilet accommodation

For many people, the accessibility of a building will be determined by the ability to locate and use the toilets. All toilet accommodation should be located and designed to allow easy use. Disabled people should be able to find and use toilets as easily as any other building users.

Wheelchair accessible unisex toilets may be designed to meet the space requirements of wheelchair users, but many other people use them. People with assistance or guide dogs, carers with children and pushchairs, people with luggage or shopping bags all express a preference for using an accessible compartment because of the additional space. Building managers should ensure that this use does not prevent disabled people from having access to a toilet. Designers should consider providing larger compartments in the general toilet accommodation for use by the above groups.

## General provision

- Doors and lobbies should be designed to allow easy access to all toilets.
- Fittings, including sanitary ware, grab rails, hand driers, coat hooks and door furniture, should contrast with their background.
- Cubicle doors should be clearly visible with visual contrast.
- Door locks, flushing controls, toilet paper dispensers, taps and all other fittings should be able to be used by people with limited manual dexterity.
- Floor finishes should be slip resistant and walls and floors should be non-shiny.
- General lighting level should be at least 100 lux.
- Cubicles, especially those with inward opening doors, should be large enough to allow comfortable use.
- In buildings used by carers and children one or more larger cubicles will allow assisted use. Approved Document M requires a larger cubicle be provided when there are four or more WC cubicles.

**Figure 4.43** WC compartments fitted for use by ambulant disabled people should always be provided.

### WC compartment for ambulant disabled people   At least one compartment in each range of male and female toilet accommodation should be designed for ambulant disabled use.

- The compartment should be at least 800 mm wide and have 750 mm activity space in front of the WC and clear of door swings.
- Door should open outwards. If the door must open inwards the length of the compartment should be increased to give at least 450 mm diameter space clear of door swing.
- There should be grab rails to both side walls, horizontal or set at 15°, 600 mm long, 680 mm above floor level with the outer end set 200 mm in front of the front edge of the WC pan.
  A 600 mm long vertical rail should be fitted to one side wall, 800 mm above floor level.
- Urinals for use by ambulant disabled people should be fitted with vertical handrails to each side.

Where cubicles or urinals are provided for ambulant disabled people or wheelchair users in the male and female toilet accommodation, all doors and lobbies should be designed to give easy access.

**Wheelchair accessible toilets**   The provision of accessible toilet facilities within a building is extremely important; it may determine whether the building is truly accessible for a disabled person.

There is no standard for the numbers of accessible toilets to be provided within a building. The recommended number will depend upon building type and use. However, wherever toilets are provided in non-domestic buildings, there should be at least one that is wheelchair accessible.

**Figure 4.44**  Good use of contrast ensures that fittings are visible, though position of bin reduces area available for side transfer.

- There should be at least one wheelchair accessible toilet provided at each location where toilets are provided for use by customers and visitors to a building, or by people working in the building.
- In working environments the horizontal travel distance to an accessible toilet should not exceed 40 m if on one floor or where the journey includes lift travel to another floor.
- Wheelchair users should not have to travel more than one storey to reach a suitable toilet if travel is via a platform lift.
- When more than one accessible toilet is provided, the layout should be handed. A tactile pictogram should indicate the handing.
- A unisex accessible toilet, accessed from a circulation area, will allow the user to be accompanied by a person of a different gender. Where an accessible compartment is provided within the standard male and female provision, this should be in addition to a unisex toilet.

> Where space is limited, for example in small business premises, a single accessible toilet could be provided instead of separate sex facilities.

- The provision of accessories available in accessible toilets should be the same as in other toilet accommodation.
- Where the wheelchair accessible toilet is the only toilet facility in a building, the width should be increased from 1500 mm to 2000 mm and a standing height washbasin should be included.

**Transfer**    Space for transfer from the wheelchair is required in front of and beside the WC. It is important that boxing-in of pipes or placing of loose fittings, such as bins, does not compromise this space.

- Where boxing-in around the cistern continues across the transfer space, the WC pan should project 750 mm to allow sufficient depth of space for side transfer.

**Figure 4.45** Projecting signage allows people to identify the position of a toilet from a distance, important for people who experience incontinence. This sign shows good use of colour contrast and symbols and, importantly, all the facilities are located in the same area.

**Figure 4.46** A clear sign with good use of colour, symbols and text. The RH identifies to a disabled person that this is a right-hand transfer toilet. This is very useful information, easily provided.

People transfer from their wheelchair from either the left- or the right-hand side, or from the front. A person who transfers from the left may be unable to use a toilet that requires transfer from the right, and vice versa.

If a toilet is to be provided in an employment situation, it is preferable to identify the needs of the disabled employee prior to carrying out the work, or to identify a location and have the money available to pay for it when needed. Putting in a toilet when the needs of a potential employee are unknown may well result in an unsatisfactory solution – and a resultant waste of money.

Service providers should be aware that if only one accessible toilet is provided within a building some disabled people might not be able to use it. Service providers may have to consider whether they have done all they reasonably can in determining the level and appropriateness of the provision available.

## Layout and dimensions

- A compartment with the standard corner toilet layout should have internal dimensions of at least 1500 mm by 2200 mm deep. The toilet is located on the rear wall, diagonally opposite the door, its centre line 500 mm from the side of the compartment and the top surface of the toilet seat 480 mm above floor level.

Accessible toilet internal dimensions of 1500 mm by 2200 mm are minimum dimensions that, in many cases, will be too small to allow easy access for wheelchair users if equipment and facilities, such as radiators, feminine hygiene machines, disposal bins, etc., are present in the compartment.

- Where the standard layout is handed the door should be handed accordingly.

**Figure 4.47**  The RADAR KEY SCHEME is used to prevent the use of accessible WC facilities by non-disabled people.

Unfortunately, while the provision of RADAR key locks is common, not all disabled people are RADAR key holders. If this facility is provided, procedures must be in place to ensure that disabled people who are not key holders, and who may wish to use the facility, can still do so. Whilst having a key available may be a management practice, adequate information on how to get the key is also essential. Long travel distances or procedures that require a lot of time to be expended in gaining access to the toilet are not acceptable.

- It is preferable that the door to the toilet opens outwards to allow access to be gained if the person using the toilet falls against the door. If the door must open inwards, minimum manoeuvring space (700 mm by 1100 mm) must exist within the toilet and suitable hinges, which allow access from the outside in an emergency, should be fitted.
- The peninsular layout allows transfer to the WC from both sides, supported by drop-down grab rails. It is recommended in

BS 8300:2001 that this layout is only used where assistance is available and should not be provided as a substitute for two separate unisex toilets with handed layouts, but as an additional facility. Minimum dimensions are 2200 mm deep by 2400 mm wide.

## Fittings and finishes

- The location of fittings such as washbasin, soap dispenser, hand drier must allow safe use from a position seated on the toilet.
- The washbasin should be fixed on the side wall of the compartment at a distance of between 140 mm and 160 mm from the front of the WC pan with a rim height of 720 mm to 740 mm. There should be no pedestal.
- Horizontal grab rails around the toilet should be set at 680 mm above the floor and provided as follows:
  - a drop-down rail to the open side of the WC, its centre line 320 mm from the centre of the WC and extending 100 mm to 150 mm beyond the front of the WC;
  - a 600 mm fixed rail on the side wall, its centre line 550 mm from the rear wall, with a 60 mm to 85 mm clearance between the rail and the wall; and
  - a fixed rail located behind the WC with a padded backrest when the cistern is in a duct or at high level.
- Vertical grab rails, at least 600 mm in length, should be set with their midpoint 1100 mm above floor level and provided as follows:
  - to the open side of the WC, its centre line 470 mm from the centre of the WC; and
  - to both sides of the washbasin, 600 mm to 700 mm apart.
- Grab rails should be easy to grip, even when wet, and securely fixed to the wall. A diameter of 32 mm to 35 mm and textured plastic coating are recommended.
- Drop-down rails should be easy to operate, and where they have a vertical support it should be set back from the front edge of the rail by at least half its length.

**Figure 4.48** The use of large floor-to-ceiling mirrors can cause confusion and should be avoided.

- A small shelf for colostomy bags should be provided close to the WC at 950 mm above floor level.
- A lever-type flush with a spatula style handle should be used, located on the transfer side of the cistern.
- Paper dispensers and other fittings should be set at a height of 800 mm to 1000 mm to their lower edge.
- Where a heated drier is provided, it should not be one that is operated by movement, it should have manual, push-button operation.
- A paper towel dispenser should always be provided for people who cannot use a heated drier.
- Fixtures and fittings, including all sanitary ware and grab rails, should contrast with their background and be clearly visible (see Plate 6 in the colour plate section).
- A horizontal rail should be fixed on the inside face of an outward opening cubicle door to enable wheelchair users to pull the door closed as they enter the compartment.
- Floor finishes should be slip resistant and walls and floors should be non-shiny as this can be visually confusing.

- Seats should be designed and fixed to allow for heavy-duty use. Gap-front seats should not be used.
- Mixer taps designed for use by people with poor grip are recommended or, where appropriate, automatic water supply can be provided.
- Feminine hygiene machines and incontinence pad dispensers should be provided adjacent to the WC. A sealed container for used incontinence pads and other disposable items should be provided, fixed securely to a wall, in a manner that does not affect the manoeuvring area within the toilet. A disposal bin for other general items should also be provided.
- Two clothes hooks should be provided at 1400 mm and 1050 mm above finished floor level.
- A small general-purpose shelf is useful, set at 700 mm height, away from the wheelchair manoeuvring area.
- A mirror should be provided above the wash hand basin that is suitable for use from seated and standing positions. A shaver point can be provided at the side of the mirror between 800 mm and 1000 mm above finished floor level.
- A full-length changing bench will be useful to some disabled people and should be incorporated where possible and/or appropriate. The bench should be located outside the minimum dimensions of the cubicle.
- Facilities, such as vending machines or shaver sockets, available in the standard WC provision, should also be available in the accessible WC. If this is not possible, perhaps due to lack of space, they should be provided in a part of the standard WC facility that is accessible to everyone.

### Emergency assistance alarm

- Accessible toilets should be fitted with emergency assistance red-coloured pull cord or other suitable device, capable of being operated from the WC or from the floor. The pull cord should be provided with two red bangles of 50 mm diameter (or open triangles with 50 mm sides), one positioned between 800 mm and 1000 mm and the other at 100 mm above the finished floor level. Alarms should be audible as well as visual and connected to a point of assistance.

- Within the accessible toilet there must be both visual and audible feedback to show that the alarm has been activated once the cord has been pulled. This is also useful if the alarm has been activated by accident, perhaps confused with a pull cord provided for the light. A reset button must be provided which can be reached when seated either on the WC or in a wheelchair.
- The alarm may be connected directly to a staffed position, for example a reception desk or security office, or may activate an alarm indicator outside the toilet compartment.

A clear written procedure must be in place for when the alarm is activated. Staff must be fully conversant with the procedure and, if the alarm indicator is sited adjacent to the accessible toilet, a notice clearly indicating what should be done if the alarm is activated should be placed on or near the compartment door. Simply opening the door from the outside without properly checking that the alarm has not been activated inadvertently could cause extreme embarrassment to the user and is not an acceptable practice.

**Figure 4.49** It can be useful and reassuring to provide information on the alarm procedure.

**Accessible urinals**   Some wheelchair users will use a urinal from a seated position or pull themselves up to use it where grab rails are provided.

- A wheelchair accessible urinal should have a rim height of 380 mm maximum and 200 mm height of clear space below. The rim should project at least 360 mm from the wall face.
- A level space 900 mm wide by 1350 mm long is needed for a wheelchair user to pull up to the urinal.
- Vertical grab rails 600 mm long should be provided on each side, 900 mm apart, height to centre line 1100 mm. A horizontal rail can be provided above the urinal.

Visual contrast between the urinal and the wall will greatly assist identification of the horizontal and vertical position of the urinal. Visual contrast at floor level is also useful. This vital information can be provided at no extra cost during a new build or in a redecoration.

Modesty panels between urinals can also help men with visual impairments orientate themselves and, if provided in addition to visual contrast, can give good, accessible provision.

**Figure 4.50** Not all disabled people use accessible toilets; some will use the standard toilet accommodation. The need for good design, colour contrast and appropriate fittings is also important here. Children should also be considered.

## Baby-changing facilities

- Baby-changing facilities should not be incorporated in wheelchair accessible toilets where there is only one accessible compartment. The compartment should be kept free for use by disabled people with separate baby-changing facilities provided in a location that is accessible to male and female carers.
- Where a nappy-changing bench is provided in an accessible compartment, it should not compromise space requirements.

> Fold-down baby-changing benches are often left in the open position and can prevent wheelchair users accessing a toilet. Careful management of such facilities, especially in toilets provided for public use, is essential.

## Facilities for working dogs

If people using working dogs are employed in, or visiting, a building an external area should be provided for the dogs to 'spend'. An area at least 2 m by 3 m should be identified with a sign such as 'For the use of working dogs only' and have a surface such as grass or bark chippings, a bin for dog waste, a supply of plastic bags and, where possible, a wash basin. There should also be procedures in place for cleaning the area.

## Changing areas

The design of changing and shower facilities should allow independent use and a choice of communal or private facilities. Many disabled people will be happy to use communal changing facilities, but some may prefer the privacy of a self-contained cubicle.

- A changing area should have at least one accessible toilet and choice of communal or private shower area.
- It is useful to include one or more unisex, self-contained, wheelchair accessible changing rooms with integral shower, WC and emergency assistance alarm.

- Lockers should be accessible to wheelchair users, with controls no higher than 1150 mm above floor level and sufficient space for approach and use. Some lockers of at least 1200 mm high should be available to take walking aids, etc.

Further guidance is given in BS 8300.

## Bathrooms and shower rooms

Bathrooms suitable for use by disabled people are required in non-domestic buildings such as hotels, halls of residence and some sports buildings. This section deals with accessible bathrooms intended for independent use only. Bathrooms in hospitals and residential homes will have specific requirements for assisted use. See BS 8300 and other relevant guidance for further information.

To allow wheelchair users and ambulant disabled people to use an accessible bathroom or shower room independently the relationship of the fittings and the space available for manoeuvring is critical. As people have differing needs a choice of bathroom layout should be provided where possible.

- All accessible bathrooms should contain a WC.
- Where only one accessible bedroom with an en-suite bathroom is provided, the bathroom should contain a shower rather than a bath, as some disabled people will be unable to use a bath.
- Where more than one accessible bedroom with en-suite facilities is provided, there should be a choice of bath or shower and a choice of left- or right-handed transfer to the WC.
- The minimum internal dimensions for a bathroom incorporating a corner WC are 2700 mm by 2500 mm and for a shower room with a corner WC are 2400 mm by 2500 mm.
- Baths should have a flat slip-resistant base, a transfer seat, a rim height of 480 mm and a horizontal or angled support rail.
- Showers should be fitted with a tip-up seat, grab rails, and a shower curtain enclosing the seat and a shelf for toiletries.
- Flooring in bathrooms and shower rooms should be slip resistant when both dry and wet.

**Figure 4.51** Bi-fold doors can be used to avoid obstructing corridors.

- Hot water temperature for bath, basin and shower should not exceed 41°C.
- An emergency assistance alarm should be provided with a pull cord reachable from the bath or shower and adjacent floor area.
- All other fittings and finishes should be as recommended for accessible WCs.

Further guidance is given in BS 8300.

# Bedrooms

Bedrooms in non-domestic buildings such as hotels, motels or student accommodation should allow easy use for as wide a range of people as possible. Wheelchair users have certain requirements for space and accessible sanitary accommodation and so a proportion of rooms should accommodate such use. Wheelchair accessible rooms should be provided in a choice of locations and on accessible routes that lead to all the other facilities within the building.

- Accessible bedrooms will require sufficient space for manoeuvre around the room and transfer to one side of the bed.
- Wheelchair users should be able to use all the facilities in the room, including balconies, and should be able to gain access to and use en-suite sanitary accommodation.
- Wheelchair users should be able to visit companions in other rooms.
- It is desirable for some accessible rooms to have a connecting door to an adjacent room for a companion or assistant.
- Accessible bedrooms should be fitted with an emergency assistance alarm operated by a pull cord that can be reached from the bed and from an adjacent floor area.

## Storage facilities

Disabled people may use storage facilities such as cupboards, shelves and lockers when at work or visiting buildings. Access to storage units, height of units and shelves, knee space and ironmongery should all be designed to allow easy use, with specific facilities provided where appropriate.

- Wherever storage facilities are provided for the general public there should be at least one fully accessible facility for disabled people.
- Wherever possible some knee spaces should be provided to allow a choice of frontal or sideways use from a sitting position.
- The corridor width between banks of storage units should be 1200 mm if some knee spaces are provided and 1400 mm if no knee spaces are provided.
- It is useful to provide some seating at storage facilities for use by ambulant disabled people.
- Ironmongery should be easy to grip and manipulate and contrast visually with its background.
- Where storage facilities are provided for a particular person, such as in a place of employment, they should be designed to suit the individual's needs.

BS 8300 contains information on reach ranges for wheelchair users and ambulant disabled people.

## Refreshment areas

Restaurants and cafeterias should be designed to be accessible in terms of both spatial design and management. Staff training is critical in areas such as these where assistance may be required to overcome design limitations.

> It may be difficult to find vending machines with all the correct requirements, but the employer or service provider should ensure that the machines they are providing are the most accessible that are available, or that they develop management procedures to assist those people who may experience difficulties when using them.
>
> There may be a temptation to remove facilities so that the provider is not discriminating against disabled people – because no one, whether disabled or non-disabled, is being provided with the service. That should not be necessary; in the vast majority of cases, careful thought and good management can overcome, or at least address, any temporary shortfall in the accessibility of products and facilities.

- Split-level areas should be linked by ramps.
- Where there are fixed tables there should be sufficient space for wheelchair users to circulate and have a choice of seating locations.
- Fixed seats will be difficult for many disabled people to use. Loose seating is preferable and can allow space for wheelchair users to pull up at tables. At least some seats should have armrests.
- Vending machines should be designed and located to allow approach and use by wheelchair users.
- Self-service counters should be continuous. Where trays need to be moved from one counter to another, assistance should be available.
- Self-service cabinets and shelves should be located within reach of wheelchair users wherever possible.

People who are deaf or hard of hearing often experience problems at cashier desks because they may be unable to follow the prices being added up and unable to hear how much is required to be paid. Simply orientating the display on the cash register so that the user can see the details of the transaction will greatly assist.

Induction loops are often of little benefit at cash register points because of the interference caused by the electrical equipment being used there.

Good lighting and staff training are essential at such points.

## Counters and service desks

Counters and service desks should accessible to wheelchair users as staff and customers.

- There should be sufficient space for wheelchair users to approach and turn towards the desk.
- The knee space and height of desk should allow close approach where this is required. Seating should be provided at low height counters.
- If there is a glazed screen it should be able to be opened to allow for direct communication. If it cannot be opened, or if there is background noise, an induction loop should be provided for the benefit of hearing aid users.
- The faces of staff employed at the counter should be well lit to allow for lip reading (see also *Reception desks*).

## Assembly areas

All assembly areas should allow access and use by disabled people as members of an audience, participants and members of staff. Disabled people should have access to the full range of seating options and be able to sit alongside disabled or non-disabled companions.

**Figure 4.52** Counters should allow communication at seated and standing heights. A low counter or low section will allow wheelchair users to communicate with staff or customers. Seats should be provided to both staff and customer side.

Guidance on seating layouts is given in *Reception areas*. In some circumstances space for lying down may be required for people who are unable to sit or stand for long periods of time.

## Lecture rooms, conference facilities, meeting rooms

- A mixture of fixed and removable seating will allow for variation in the number of wheelchair users accommodated.
- Provision should be made for wheelchair users as members of the audience and speakers.
- Any raised area or podium should be wheelchair accessible.
- Lecterns and other fittings and controls should allow use at a variety of heights.
- Good sight lines and lighting are particularly important to allow for lip reading and the interpretation of sign language.

- A hearing enhancement system should be provided. These systems are described in *Communication and wayfinding.*

## Lecture rooms with raked floors

- Wheelchair spaces should be provided in a choice of spaces and should be provided with a handrail and crash bar at any change of level.
- Access routes should be provided with handrails.

## Auditoria, stadia and spectator seating

- Disabled people should have access to the full range of seating locations and be able to sit alongside a disabled or non-disabled companion.
- Routes should be accessible and of sufficient width to allow wheelchair users and ambulant disabled people to circulate.
- Handrails should always be provided to stepped and ramped routes.
- Numbers of spaces for wheelchair users should be in accordance with the guidance given in BS 8300 and Approved Document M. In addition, there should be transfer seats provided for wheelchair users who wish to transfer from their wheelchair to a seat for the duration of the performance.
- Space should be available for working dogs adjacent to seating and clear of circulation routes.
- Wheelchair seating areas in sports stadia should be designed to allow wheelchair users to see the event even when people in front stand up.
- All wheelchair seating locations should have access to an accessible unisex toilet.
- A hearing enhancement system should be provided.
- Emergency egress procedures should take account of the needs of all people who need assistance, whether they are seated in designated areas or not.

**Sports venues**   Facilities should be provided at sports venues to allow disabled people to participate and compete in all the available sports. Guidance on circulation and provision of facilities should be followed.

- Sports wheelchairs are often wider and longer than standard wheelchairs and so additional circulation space is required. Door widths and lift sizes should be increased.
- There should be level access from changing facilities to sports areas and swimming pools.
- Access into swimming pools should be provided with a choice of methods, such as ramped access or hoist.
- Hearing enhancement should be provided in fitness and exercise areas where instruction may be given to participants.

A radio receiver system is often used in sports stadia to provide an audio description service for spectators.

**Figure 4.53** A low counter, fitted with an induction loop, can help provide easy access.

## Controls and equipment

**Ease of use**   All building users should be able to operate the controls and equipment provided for their use. Ease of operation depends upon these items:

- being within reach;
- not requiring excessive strength or dexterity;
- having clear instructions for use that are visible, and where appropriate audible and/or tactile.

**Coin and card operated devices**   Coin and card operated devices such as vending machines and automatic teller machines (ATMs) should be designed and located to allow easy independent use.

- The height of controls should allow access from a seated or standing position, with knee space provided where possible to allow wheelchair users to pull up facing the front of the device.
- Controls should allow use by people with limited manual dexterity and sensory impairments.
- Display screens should be visible and shaded to prevent glare and reflection.
- Clear operating instructions should be provided.

**Building services – sockets, switches and controls**
Building service controls should be designed and located to be able to be seen and used easily. Ideally, controls such as switches and sockets should be located consistently throughout a building at a height within the reach range of all users.

- Controls should not require the use of both hands simultaneously.
- Controls should visually contrast with their background and have embossed tactile information where appropriate.
- The use of large touch plates and rocker switches will benefit people with visual impairments and limited manual dexterity.

> Light switches will be easier to locate when entering a room if they are aligned horizontally with the door handle.

- Wall-mounted socket outlets, telephone points and TV sockets should be located between 400 mm and 1000 mm above the floor with a preference for the lower end of the range. Socket outlets should be no nearer than 350 mm to room corners.
- Switches for permanently wired appliances should be located between 400 mm and 1200 mm above the floor.
- All switches and controls requiring precise hand movements should be between 750 mm and 1200 mm above the floor.
- Simple push-button controls should be not more than 1200 mm above the floor, though light switches for use by the general public should be located between 900 mm and 1100 mm and have large push pads.
- Controls that need close vision should be between 1200 mm and 1400 mm above the floor to allow use by both seated and standing users.

**Alarms**   The design of alarm systems within buildings should take account of the needs of all building users. Alarm activation should be able to be carried out by wheelchair users. People with hearing impairments should be aware that alarms have been set of or announcements made.

- Where audible alarms are used they should be supplemented with visual systems if located in areas where people with hearing impairments are likely to be alone.
- Personal vibrating pagers can also be used to supplement an alarm system.
- Alarm call points should be located within reach of seated and standing users and designed to allow easy use.
- Alarm pull cords should be coloured red, located as close to a wall as possible and have two red 50 mm diameter (or open triangle) bangles, one at 100 mm and one between 800 mm and 1000 mm above the floor.

Vibrating pagers can be useful and cost effective, especially if required by only a few people using a building. However, there are management implications that need to be considered, such as ongoing testing and the replacement or recharging of batteries.

In addition, there will be issues of how and when the pager will be used. For example, pagers that attach to a belt are unlikely to be easily usable by everyone. Pagers need to have direct contact with the person using them to be effective; those placed in handbags, jacket pockets or in desk drawers are very unlikely to be of any use.

Supplying pagers is not sufficient – providing ones appropriate to the needs of the user is essential, as is good management of the whole process to make sure it works effectively.

- Where emergency assistance alarms are located in toilets, bathrooms, changing rooms or hotel bedrooms, there should be visible and audible feedback to indicate the alarm has been activated.
- Emergency assistance alarm indicators should be located where they will be seen and heard by those able to give assistance.

**Windows and window controls**    The location of windows and window controls and the ease of use of controls will affect the ability of people to use windows effectively. An appropriate sill height and controls that are easily operated and located within reach will allow wheelchair users, ambulant disabled people and others to use windows independently.

- Window furniture should be visible and located within reach.
- Window controls for independent use by disabled people should be located between 800 mm and 1000 mm above the floor.
- Controls should be able to be used without excessive strength.
- Powered systems can be used to eliminate the need for manual opening and closing.

In many window designs, a fanlight is incorporated to allow a small amount of ventilation. When it is raining, using a fanlight may be essential as open casements may allow water to penetrate into the room.

The opening mechanism to any fanlight should be placed within easy reach of all users, or another suitable method of opening provided.

Window controls that require the user to climb to operate them, for example when fitted furniture is located in front of the window, must be avoided. Remote opening either by a manual or powered means should be provided.

## Communication and wayfinding

Building design can help or hinder communication. The use of lighting, visual contrast, signs, hearing enhancement systems and

**Figure 4.54** Visual contrast can be used to assist orientation and identify features.

the provision of information in a variety of formats will all affect the ability of people to use a building independently. It is not just people with sensory impairments who benefit from good design in these areas; it is everyone.

## Access to information

It is important that people have access to information, including signs, leaflets and verbal information.

Most information in buildings is given visually, but the use of other senses should be considered and acoustic, tactile and olfactory factors incorporated into building design. A sound such as a water feature may be a useful landmark in a large office building. A person with a visual impairment might use the sound of lift doors or an activity taking place at a counter to assist in locating the service.

- A high level of background noise should be avoided where possible as it can cut out useful noises that may help with navigation.

Tactile signs or maps will be useful to some people, if located where they can be found and touched. See *Signs* and *Tactile surfaces* for further information.

Olfaction is a valuable source of information, currently underutilised inside buildings, that can aid navigation if used appropriately.

- Cedar and other woods used in building have a distinctive smell and fragrant plants can also be used to provide pleasure and orientation clues for people with visual impairments.
- Air movement and temperature can also give useful clues to help with orientation.

Environments that encourage feelings of comfort and wellbeing are important. The use of a variety of sensory information can make environments more pleasurable for everyone, as well as providing useful information to people with visual impairments.

## Visible reinforcement

- Answerphone systems, bells and buzzers should have visible indicators to confirm their operation.
- Public address systems should also give visible information using, for example, an LED screen to supplement the audible message.
- Alarm systems should also take into account the needs of people with hearing impairments and should be backed up by visible confirmation.

### Written information

- Leaflets should use clear print and information should be provided in other formats where necessary. This could include tactile maps, information in Braille or on audiotape.

It can be very useful to visitors to provide information about the accessibility of a building in advance of a visit. An access leaflet with information on public transport, parking arrangements and facilities available within the building will allow disabled visitors to plan their visit and be aware in advance of any potential problem areas. This information itself should be available in a variety of formats.

Not all literature has to be printed in accessible style and type – but accessible formats, including large print and audiotape, must be available if requested. Information in Braille may not always be necessary because people who read Braille may also be able to get the information they need using an audiotape. However, if required, it should be provided.

# Wayfinding

Building layout affects wayfinding. A logical straightforward layout will allow people to navigate more easily, remember routes and can assist means of escape. The wayfinding process is dependent upon receiving and processing information; the more quickly and accurately people are able to do this, the more rapidly the journey will be completed.

When living in and moving through environments, most people use the five senses of sight, hearing, touch, smell and taste to gain information. It has been estimated that 70–75% of information people receive is through vision and that 10–15% comes through hearing. The remainder is gathered through the remaining senses.

For people who have significant sight loss, the 70–75% of visual information will be reduced, and completely eliminated in the case of those who are totally blind. However, the problem is not restricted to people with visual impairments. Anyone with more than minor hearing loss will need to obtain information through visual clues, so that they can avoid having to ask for directions, knowing that they would have difficulty in hearing the reply.

- Signs, colour and contrasting tactile information can all be used to help with navigation.
- Colour can be used to identify routes or differentiate between areas or storeys of buildings.
- Visual contrast can help distinguish surfaces and features.
- Tactile information can be given by floor surfaces, embossing on signs or the provision of maps and models that enable visitors with visual impairments to understand a building shape and layout.
- Audio guides can be provided, as in some visitor attractions.

**Tactile surfaces**    Tactile paving can impart useful information when used correctly. A number of different profiles have been developed, each of which has a specific meaning. Care should be taken to install the appropriate texture, colour and hardness.

- The most commonly seen pattern is the modified blister, which is used externally at dropped kerbs or raised road surfaces to indicate the edge of the pavement. Different colours indicate the presence of a controlled or uncontrolled crossing.
- The hazard warning pattern, corduroy with a half-rod-shaped profile, is used at the top and bottom of stairs.
- A flat-topped ribbed profile denotes a guidance path; this can be used in large open areas such as pedestrian precincts.
- Non-specific changes of profile and texture in internal and external surfaces can be used to give general information on routes and to guide people clear of hazards in circulation areas.

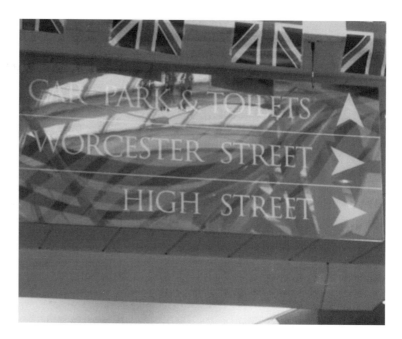

**Figure 4.55** The incorrect use of surface finish can completely negate the effectiveness of a sign, especially in certain lighting situations. Non-reflective surface finishes for signs are essential.

- Tactile features can also be used on signs, maps, controls and handrails.

**Human interaction**   The attitude adopted by those managing an environment, often first encountered at a car park entrance, reception or help desk, can have a major impact on the accessibility of an environment for all users, but especially disabled people.

Staff should be trained to understand the needs of particular user groups, how to communicate effectively and how to offer assistance when required. This is often a very cost-effective way of improving dramatically the way in which disabled people can safely, effectively and independently use an environment.

- Management responses to requests for assistance to use an external lift, approach or enter a building, should be devised, practised by staff and operable at all times.
- Where a control device contains an audible communication system, to announce arrival or seek assistance, the needs of

people who are deaf or hard of hearing must be considered. Clear information should be given at the control device and a management response available at all times.

- Staff should be trained in dealing with the communication needs of people who are deaf or hard of hearing.
- Reception staff should know of the location of facilities such as accessible toilets.
- Key staff should understand the needs of people with visual impairments and undergo basic mobility training to assist them in moving around an environment safely if required.
- Key staff should be trained in clear speaking and, if possible, basic sign language, to assist people who are deaf or hard of hearing.
- Staff should be fully trained in the use of any mobility equipment, such as platform lifts. Records should be kept of who has been trained and assistance should be available at all times.
- Visitors should be informed when there is assistance available.
- Staff should be aware of the potential problems of certain actions, such as the use of home-made temporary signs that do not follow good practice design guidance or the positioning of obstacles in circulation spaces.
- In existing buildings where access barriers may be difficult to eliminate completely, staff input will be critical.

---

The importance of good staff training and the ability of staff to be able to recognise that a difficulty may exist, and to be able to move swiftly, and appropriately, to address the issue cannot be overemphasised.

Not all buildings are accessible. Disabled people know this and most acknowledge that not everything can be perfect. However, what is important to them is to be able to experience an equal opportunity to that experienced by non-disabled people. The interface between staff and disabled and non-disabled users of a service is critical in how imperfections in an environment are dealt with, and whether the obstacle met is acceptable or unacceptable, surmountable or insurmountable.

**Signs**   If a building is designed in a logical and simple manner, the need for signs is minimised. The design of the external environment should lead people to the entrance and internally there should be clear, logical routes and access to services. Where signs are needed, they should be well placed, well lit and use clearly visible print.

Signs are of particular importance to people who are deaf or hard of hearing, who often will not ask for directions, as they may be unable to hear the answer. Signs will also benefit older people, those with learning difficulties or short-term memory loss, who may need reassurance they have taken, and are still on, the correct route.

Well-contrasted, correctly sized signs with lower case lettering and, where appropriate, tactile (embossed or Braille) information will also assist those with restricted vision. Colour coding and

**Figure 4.56** Signs should be clear and easy to understand. Too many signs can cause confusion. Effective, ongoing management of signage is essential.

symbols can be useful if used consistently (see Plate 7 in the colour plate section).

However, in reality, all users will benefit from a signage system that is well designed and properly co-ordinated.

- Signs should be simple, short and easily understood.
- Signs should be consistent, using prescribed typefaces and graphic devices.
- Capitalised lower case lettering is generally easier to read.
- The typeface used should be clearly legible and preferably sans serif.
- The number of different typefaces and font sizes on a sign should be kept to a minimum.
- The size of lettering should be appropriate to the distance from which the sign is viewed.
- The signboard should contrast with its background and the lettering should contrast with the signboard (see Plate 8 in the colour plate section).

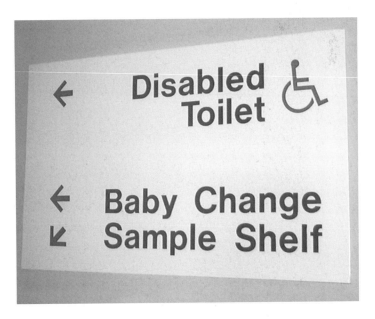

**Figure 4.57** Good clear signage, though the word Disabled is unnecessary. Toilet or WC accompanied by the symbol is sufficient.

**Figure 4.58** Good use of text, contrast, symbols and directional arrows – and ideally sized, bearing in mind the distance from which it will be viewed.

If signs have visual contrast with their background, this can be particularly helpful to visually impaired people and also to make them more readily identifiable for people who are deaf or hard of hearing. The latter group rely heavily on signage for information, as they are often reluctant to ask directions in case they will be unable to hear or decipher the response.

- Light lettering set on a dark background is generally easier to read.
- Locating signs at eye level with easy access for close viewing will benefit everyone.
- To avoid glare signboards should be non-reflective and lighting positioned appropriately.
- The use of appropriately positioned tactile maps or plans can be of benefit to all users, but especially those with restricted vision. Tactile signs should be positioned where they can be easily reached. Tactile information should be embossed between 1 mm and 1.5 mm.
- Information in Braille should be used in addition to embossed information, not instead of, and should be kept to the minimum required.

The number of people who read Braille is small compared
with the number who would benefit from the appropriate use
of well-designed embossed lettering, numbers or symbols.
In addition, the way that Braille is normally 'read', i.e.
horizontally at table or lap position, means that providing
too much Braille on a vertical sign will actually be difficult
to read and, in most cases of little benefit to Braille readers.
More useful would be to provide clear, well-designed
embossed signs, accompanied by a limited amount of
Braille to identify what features the sign is identifying.

   If larger amounts of information are needed in Braille,
the delivery of it, in terms of positioning and design of
the signboard, needs to be carefully considered.

- Symbols can be very useful, particularly where decisions need to be taken quickly, such as in transport environments.
- It may be necessary to complement symbols by text to clearly define their meaning; for example, a wheelchair symbol can be used to signify an accessible toilet, an accessible route or parking space.

**Figure 4.59** Symbols can be useful for many people.

Ideally any signs should incorporate a combination of lettering and symbols.

Symbols are useful for people who experience dyslexia, those with learning disabilities and people who do not speak or understand the language of the sign. For some people with learning disabilities, information may be given totally in symbols.

As a general recommendation, specialist publications should be consulted on the design and layout of signs, and specialist designers should be employed to advise on the most appropriate signage to use.

- Lighting should ensure that signs could be seen when daylight is poor.

Detailed information on signs is given in Sign Design Guide (Sign Design Society, JMU 2000).

**Figure 4.60** The use of the letters WC indicates this is an accessible toilet. Using the symbol without the letters may suggest to some people that this an area related to disability, but not necessarily a toilet.

## Lighting

Good lighting is important for everyone. Lighting can be used to enhance visual contrast to increase the visibility of routes and objects and make environments more easily legible and safer to use.

The design of a building or environment should allow people with visual impairments to use the vision they have as well as providing the other factors that can assist navigation. Older people and people with visual impairments generally require higher lighting levels. Good levels of lighting are also required to allow people to lip read or use sign language.

People with visual impairments are generally sensitive to glare and have longer adaptation times than people without a visual impairment. Adaptation is the process by which the visual system changes to optimise viewing in either a darker or lighter environment. In general, moving from a dark environment to a bright environment, such as may occur when walking out of a building on a bright sunny day, or in an emergency situation when the mains electrical supply fails and emergency lighting, normally at a much reduced level, is provided, will present few problems for people who do not have a visual impairment. However, for people with a visual impairment, adaptation times are greatly extended.

Designing lighting systems to meet the requirements of an inclusive environment is possible with modern technology. When the design is based on the needs of people with visual impairments, the needs of all other users will normally be met. Controlling glare and diversity or uniformity within a space has the potential to assist all users.

- General lighting should be controllable and adjustable to meet individual requirements.
- Good lighting is critical where there are potential hazards such as changes of level.
- Light sources should be located to avoid glare, reflection and strong shadows.
- Lighting can be used to help identify features and objects by emphasising shape, form and texture.

**Figure 4.61** Strong shadows can cause confusion and make navigation difficult.

• Good lighting is important to allow communication by lip reading and sign language.

At a reception desk, cashier point or at any point where people may be required to complete forms or read or understand instructions, an ability to be able to control the lighting available in given circumstances is critical.

Control may be by way of providing switches which can increase or lower the amount of main lighting available, additional lighting which can be switched on when needed or by the provision of a task light. However, it is important to remember that because such a provision may not be in constant use, the switch to operate it must not be placed in some inaccessible position. When needed it may be needed swiftly, and accessible switching and good staff training are essential.

- There is no definitive guidance on lighting levels for people with visual impairments as their needs vary widely. However, lighting levels of between 25% and 50% above those given in CIBSE guidance are generally recommended.
- Where possible, windows should not be positioned where they allow glare and reflection from sunlight on stairs, corridors and other areas. The position of the windows may not be able to be altered, but window blinds could be fitted or films applied to the glass where appropriate.
- Task lighting should be controllable and adjustable to meet individual requirements. Illumination requirements will vary depending upon the task to be undertaken and the relative brightness of the surfaces within the space being lit. Some people, because of the nature of their visual impairment, work close to a task light and so lights that generate a lot of heat should be avoided.
- Fluorescent lighting can cause a hum in hearing aids and should be used with care to minimise inconvenience to hearing aid users.

**Figure 4.62** Window blinds or shading can be used to control natural lighting and prevent strong shadows and glare.

## Visual contrast and light reflectance values

Visual contrast used in decoration gives information to building users and can be of particular importance to people with visual impairments. For people with adequate vision, differences in hue (the nature of the colour) and chroma (the intensity of the colour) provide sufficient visual contrast. For people with impaired vision, it appears that the amount of light that a surface reflects, the light reflectance value (LRV), is the main feature that identifies differences in colour. Differences in LRV should be used to assess the degree of visual contrast between surfaces and features. For example, the LRV of a wall should be noticeably different from that of a ceiling and of a floor.

Information on light reflectance values is given in the publication A Design Guide for the Use of Colour and Contrast to Improve the Built Environment for Visually Impaired People (ICI Paints 1997) and in BS 8300.

Visual contrast will assist most people, especially those with visual impairments, at certain points. These fall into two categories, which can best be described as those that are critical surfaces and those that are special features. Critical surfaces are large areas that, when scanned by a visually impaired person, form the impression of space, shape and proximity. Examples are ceilings, walls, doors, floors and stairs.

Special features are additional areas, smaller than critical features, that need to be highlighted to allow the building to be used easily by people with visual impairments. Such features include sanitary ware, handrails and stair nosing, door handles and socket outlets, all of which should be contrasted with the background against which they will be seen.

- The size and shape of a feature is an important clue to its identity. There are few features within a building that offer the same visual image, in terms of size and shape, as a door adequately contrasted with its surroundings.
- Navigating through a building is much easier if critical surfaces are visually contrasted.

- On critical surfaces the use of highly reflective, shiny finishes can cause considerable confusion for everyone. Such finishes should be used with caution.
- Trim items, such as coving, skirting, architrave, dado rail, etc., should be decorated in colours that maintain or improve the impact of the colours used on the larger critical surfaces.
- Special features such as sanitary ware, handrails, stair nosings, door handles, socket outlets and switches should be contrasted with the background against which they will be seen.

Colours for use in buildings may be specified using BS 4800, which gives a schedule of 100 colours, in conjunction with BS 5252, which gives a framework for colour coordination and has available a colour-matching fan.

**Identifying hazards**   The vast majority of people with visual impairments say that colliding with furniture and obstacles in the walking area is a frequent and disconcerting occurrence.

Obstacles that are free standing, project from walls or overhead should be kept to a minimum and adequately contrasted with the critical surface against which they will be viewed.

Visual contrast, especially when related to the identification of hazards, is equally as important for people who are deaf and hard of hearing as it is to those with restricted visual ability.

To communicate with other people when walking or moving around, people who are deaf or hard of hearing will often look at the person they are communicating with to lip read or to sign. When doing this, they will be relying on their peripheral vision where, just as with a visually impaired person, their ability to see colour and fine detail is poor. Deaf people can, and do, trip over and collide with hazards, not because their vision is poor, but because their strategy for communication means they are not always looking in the direction they are going. But doesn't that happen to most people at some time or another?

## Acoustic environment

The acoustic environment is critical to allow people to use their hearing capability effectively. Many people with hearing impairments will use lip reading and so visual conditions are important also.

- The acoustic environment will affect the ability to communicate, as will light levels.
- The reduction of background noise is beneficial; however, some reflected sound can assist people with visual impairments in understanding the space that they are in and to hear others approaching them.
- Lighting and visibility should be sufficient to allow lip reading.
- Hearing enhancement systems: induction loops, infrared systems, radio systems, can be useful where information is given verbally.
- Key staff should be trained in communicating and interacting with deaf and hard of hearing people. The 'hearing aware' symbol can be used where trained staff are available.

**Hearing enhancement systems**    Electronic hearing enhancement is used in buildings to amplify sound or to provide additional information to users. The two most common types are induction loops and infrared systems, though radio transmitters are also used where appropriate. Standard signs should always be used to inform of the presence of these systems.

Effective use of hearing enhancement systems relies on maintenance and management procedures. Potential users need to be aware that a system exists, hence the need for signs, and staff should be able to operate the system. All equipment should be regularly checked and maintained.

It is important that equipment, such as an induction loop installation, is properly maintained and tested. To be of use it must be working when the disabled person needs to use it.

**Induction loops**    Induction loops transfer sound spoken into a microphone into sound for transmission to a hearing aid. Induction loops work by converting sound via a microphone into a varying magnetic field that is converted back to amplified sound by an individual's hearing aid. They are commonly used at reception desks, counters and in meeting rooms.

- The hearing aid should be set to a 'T' position to pick up the amplified sound and so it is important that the presence of the induction loop is indicated.
- Induction loops only benefit hearing aid users and so there is still a need for good communication skills and clear written instructions as appropriate.
- An induction loop can be built into a room or counter and portable induction loop systems are also available.

---

The provision of induction loops needs careful consideration if money is not to be wasted on inappropriate installations. In shops, induction loops positioned at tills are unlikely to be of significant value because of interference from electrical equipment such as cash registers. Simply orientating the cash display so that someone who is deaf or hard of hearing can actually see the totals may often be the better, more appropriate, solution.

However, there will be areas where the need to transfer information clearly is essential, for example at a pharmaceutical counter where important information about the taking of drugs is being given. Here, the need for an induction loop to ensure instructions are fully understood could be critical.

---

**Infrared systems**    In an infrared system, a microphone is used to collect sound, which is sent to an amplifier and coder that converts the sound into infrared light. The receivers, usually headsets, convert the light into sound information to transmit to the wearer. Infrared systems are used in theatres, lecture rooms and other controlled environments where it is possible to manage the supply and collection of receivers.

**Radio systems**    Radio receiver hearing enhancement systems are portable as users carry personal receivers and are often used in schools and colleges where students move between classrooms. They are also used in sports stadia to provide a commentary to spectators. Information can be transmitted on more than one channel.

**Telephones**    Where public telephones are provided in a building at least one should be accessible for wheelchair users. Where there is a selection of telephones with different payment methods one of each type should be available to wheelchair users.

- Where there is only one public telephone it can be set at a low height provided a seat (fold down if necessary) is available.
- The maximum height of the top control or slot should be no more than 1200 mm above the floor.
- To assist people who may need to steady themselves when using the telephone a support rail should be fixed to the wall adjacent.
- A shelf should be provided for use of a portable text phone.
- Any instructions should be provided in formats suitable for people with visual impairments.
- Public telephones should be fitted with inductive couplers and a variable volume control.
- Wherever possible, a text phone should be provided for public use.
- Any sound covers used must allow access by all users and not be hazardous to people with visual impairments.

# Emergency egress

Egress must be considered alongside access. A well-designed, accessible building should allow independent egress for as many of its occupants as possible. Safe, efficient egress will depend upon a combination of management procedures and building design.

Specific evacuation strategies may need to be devised for people who need assistance, for example where lifts cannot be used for vertical escape. These strategies should take into account the building design, the known needs of people working in a building, as well as the unknown needs of visitors.

Fire engineering techniques can be used to assess the risk of fire in any part of a building, taking into account factors such as compartmentation, intelligent alarm systems, sprinklers and smoke control. This can provide the basis for an evacuation strategy for a particular building with a particular pattern of use.

It is important to provide people with the information necessary to allow them to make informed choices. Clear warnings, signs and instructions are needed to tell people where to go and what to do in an emergency. Disabled people are often well aware of personal risk management and are more likely than others to act rationally if provided with the appropriate information.

**Generic evacuation plans**    The needs of visitors to a building may not be known and a generic plan should be devised to deal with the evacuation of people who may need assistance. A plan of this sort should consider the needs of wheelchair users, ambulant disabled people, people with sensory impairments and others whose needs cannot be identified in advance.

**Personal emergency egress plans**    Personal emergency egress plans (PEEPs) should be devised for employees who have specific needs.

- The plan should take into account the building design and how it may cause difficulties in evacuation, the type of assistance required to overcome these difficulties and any other requirements specific to that employee.
- Where assistance is required, the plan should also set out how and by whom that assistance will be given.

**Horizontal and vertical evacuation**    Horizontal and vertical evacuation should be considered. Some people may be able to evacuate themselves horizontally to a fire-protected refuge space, on or near to escape stairs, but need assistance to facilitate vertical escape. If an evacuation lift is not available, people may need to be carried down stairs. Evacuation chairs can be used in this situation. These are lightweight chairs that can be operated by one person, rather than the three people required to carry a wheelchair and occupant. However, evacuation chairs may not be suitable for all wheelchair users and some people may prefer to be carried in their wheelchairs.

The use of phased evacuation in larger buildings, where people are initially transferred to a separate compartment within the building and then evacuated vertically, may allow lifts to be used for vertical escape.

**Refuges**    A refuge is defined by BS 5588 Part 8 as an 'area that is enclosed with fire resisting construction and served directly by a safe route to a storey exit, evacuation lift or final exit, thus constituting a temporary safe place for disabled people to await assistance for their evacuation'. The BS goes on to say that refuges are relatively safe waiting areas for short periods. They are not areas where disabled people should be left indefinitely until rescued by the fire service, or until the fire is extinguished.

**Figure 4.63** Refuges should be clearly identified and a system of communication provided.

- Refuges should be identified and clearly signposted.
- Size and location of refuges need to be carefully considered. It is preferable to locate refuges on escape routes, where people using the refuge can be seen.
- There should be a two-way communication system provided to allow a person waiting in the refuge to communicate with those organising the evacuation. It is preferable to provide a visual link as well as verbal as this allows for checking refuge occupancy in an emergency situation.
- Where escape is via stairs, evacuation chairs should be provided in the refuge and staff trained to operate the chairs.

**Assistance**    Availability of assistance must be considered. Where a disabled employee has a personal emergency egress plan the assistance need is known in advance and can be planned for. The needs of visitors will not always be known and strategies must be developed to accommodate their evacuation needs.

- Where a horizontal evacuation strategy includes the use of refuges there should be planned procedures for assisted vertical evacuation.
- It is the responsibility of the building management, not the fire brigade, to evacuate people.
- Management should carry out staff training, regular reviews of plans and organise regular practices.
- There should be regular checking of escape routes and fire alarm and fire-fighting equipment.

**Evacuation lifts**    Multi-storey buildings should be provided with at least one evacuation lift. This is a lift with an independent power supply and control and located in a fire-protected shaft that can be used for emergency evacuation.

**Fire alarm systems and equipment**    The fire alarm system in a building should be suitable for everyone. Issues to be considered should include the type and location of manual call points, whether an automatic detection system is required and the addition of visual alarms to an audible alarm system.

- Manual call points should be located where they can be reached by everyone, including wheelchair users, and consideration should be given to providing alternative types of call mechanisms, such as pull cords.
- Audible alarm systems should be supplemented by visual means of warning for people with hearing impairments. The use of individual vibrating warning devices may also be appropriate.
- Fire extinguishers, fire alarm call devices, hoses, blankets and other equipment should be positioned to allow everyone to reach, take down and use.
- There should be clear instructions on emergency procedures and clear signs.

**Emergency lighting**   There is a need for emergency lighting to be provided in many buildings and the usual approach is to adopt the requirements of BS 5266. This is generally concerned with overhead lighting. Where visually impaired people are likely to use the escape route, more than the minimum 0.2 lux recommendation of BS 5266 should be provided. It is recommended that visually impaired people be provided with a minimum of 3 lux along the escape route.

In addition, there are also a variety of wayguidance systems available, which may offer an important contribution to escape efficiency in situations where the evacuation of large numbers of

**Figure 4.64** Fire exit signs should be located where they are clearly visible and care taken to ensure lighting does not cause reflections that obscure the information.

people may be required, for example, from buildings such as auditoria, theatres or cinemas.

Unpowered photoluminescent wayguidance systems are not currently recommended for use in areas where visually impaired people have access. In this system, a photoluminescent material, perhaps in the shape of strips or blocks, absorbs light from the main lighting system when in general use and emits it after the main lighting has gone out. The amount of light provided by the system has been found to be too low to be identified by visually impaired people.

Powered wayguidance systems are generally mounted at low level and provide a strip of continuous light or a strip of closely spaced individual light sources, such as light emitting diodes (LEDs). Although powered wayguidance systems are relatively new, they are becoming more available.

**Figure 4.65** The use of powered wayguidance systems will not be appropriate in all buildings in all situations. However, in buildings where there may be a need to evacuate a lot of people (disabled and non-disabled), such as from cinemas, auditoria, conference venues, etc., the selective use of such systems can assist considerably in improving the evacuation speed of all users.

**Figure 4.66** Assisting disabled people out of the building using a fire exit with external steps presents management issues that simply cannot be addressed by an *ad hoc* escape policy.

**Final exit**    Exit routes and exit doors should be accessible to all disabled people, including wheelchair users. Steps at final exits must be avoided if possible. Thresholds should be level and doors should be wide enough to allow a disabled person to pass through to an equal standard as when entering the building.

Exit arrangements are often overlooked in access audits or not considered in sufficient detail. Where there is no proper assisted escape procedure and it is necessary for a disabled person to be physically lifted to overcome even one step at the exit, there could be serious ramifications for the managers of the building, not to mention the disabled person.

For example, lifting a wheelchair with a disabled person in it may well subject employees to an action which is contrary to that permitted under other legislation, such as health and safety or lifting regulations. Staff may well seek compensation if a management practice such as this causes injury to them. The person using the wheelchair may be injured in the lifting process and may also seek compensation.

Wherever there are steps, internally or externally, a refuge should be provided and an assisted escape procedure devised, regularly reviewed and updated.

# Appendix A
# General acceptability criteria

## Access audit checklists

The following checklists have been prepared as an example of easy reference guides that can be used when undertaking access audits.

The questions identified here are the more general issues of the type that should always be considered in an audit. There may well be others that also need to be considered in individual situations.

Checklists such as the ones described here should only be used as an 'aide mémoire', a method of recording information and a way of highlighting issues. They should never be used as the sole method of reporting on access issues to a client.

## How to use the checklists

When using the checklist, circle the response in the ✓ column for yes or in the ✗ column for no.

If the question contains the words 'if any' and none is provided – do not respond to the question.

Only respond to one of the questions posed in those which offer an OR response.

Respond to both questions for those which offer an AND response.

Sometime you are just asked to circle the ✗ if something exists. That is because there is definitely an access issue that needs to be considered and there is further information elsewhere in the Manual or, in some cases, BS 8300 or Approved Document M of the Building Regulations.

If one of the items described in the checklist achieves a ✗, then issues will need to be addressed and, probably, some work needs to be carried out. This may be physical alterations or changes in terms of practices, policies or management procedures.

affl = above finished floor level.

## Accessible car parking checklist

| Item | Check | |
|---|:---:|:---:|
| **Signage** | | |
| The position of the designated accessible car parking bays is clearly signed from the entrance to the car park | ✓ | ✗ |
| Appropriate signage (symbol) is provided at ground level (white or yellow and at least 1400 mm high) | ✓ | ✗ |
| Appropriate signage (text and symbol) is provided vertically at the back of each bay which is high enough to be seen when the accessible bay is occupied | ✓ | ✗ |
| **Position of bays** | | |
| The accessible parking bays are sited as close to the main entrance of the building as is practicable | ✓ | ✗ |
| The travel distance from the accessible bays to the main entrance (or the accessible entrance) is less than 50 metres | ✓ | ✗ |
| If the travel distance is greater than 50 metres, the route is undercover | ✓ | ✗ |
| Circle ✗ if the travel distance is greater than 100 metres | | ✗ |
| The bays are positioned appropriately relative to the slope, if any, of the site between the accessible bay and the main accessible entrance | ✓ | ✗ |
| **Number of bays** | | |
| The number of bays provided is appropriate to the use of the building or buildings | ✓ | ✗ |
| **Size of bays** | | |
| If a single accessible parking bay is provided, it is a minimum of 4800 mm long by 3600 mm (including a 1200 mm transfer zone) | ✓ | ✗ |
| OR | | |
| If a bank of accessible parking bays is provided each bay is at least 4800 mm long by 2400 mm wide with an additional transfer zone of 1200 mm between bays | ✓ | ✗ |
| The minimum size of standard parking bays is at least 4800 mm by 2400 mm | ✓ | ✗ |
| There is a suitable marked zone at the end of each bay to allow entry and egress from the rear of a vehicle | ✓ | ✗ |
| **Pedestrian routes** | | |
| Routes through the car park are clearly signed | ✓ | ✗ |
| Routes through the car park are clearly defined using texture or colour | ✓ | ✗ |
| Routes through the car park are wide enough | ✓ | ✗ |
| Routes through the car park are free from hazards | ✓ | ✗ |
| Routes through the car park are slip resistant (including when wet) | ✓ | ✗ |
| Routes through the car park are likely to be free from puddles when wet | ✓ | ✗ |
| Profile paving (blister) is provided at dropped kerbs | ✓ | ✗ |

| Item | Check | |
|---|---|---|
| **Surface finish** | | |
| The surface finish to all car parking areas and setting down points (if any) is firm | ✓ | ✗ |
| The surface finish to all car parking areas and setting down points (if any) is well maintained | ✓ | ✗ |
| Open joints between paving slabs (if any) do not exceed 10 mm | ✓ | ✗ |
| Maximum difference in level of paving slabs (if any) does not exceed 5 mm | ✓ | ✗ |
| **Lighting** | | |
| Lighting is provided to the car park | ✓ | ✗ |
| Lighting is provided to the setting down point (if any) | ✓ | ✗ |
| Lighting is well maintained | ✓ | ✗ |
| Lighting, in terms of illuminance and provision, is appropriate | ✓ | ✗ |
| **Setting down point** | | |
| A setting down point at least 6600 mm long is provided as close as practicable to the main accessible entrance | ✓ | ✗ |
| The setting down point is appropriately signed | ✓ | ✗ |
| There is a level kerb | ✓ | ✗ |
| A shelter is provided | ✓ | ✗ |
| There is an appropriate procedure in place to manage the use of the setting down point | ✓ | ✗ |
| **Management** | | |
| There are appropriate procedures in place to manage the accessible parking bays and setting down points | ✓ | ✗ |
| Ticket machines (if any) are fully accessible to disabled people | ✓ | ✗ |
| **Generally** | | |
| Methods of controlling entry to the car park are suitable for all potential disabled users | ✓ | ✗ |

## External areas checklist

| Item | Check | |
|---|:---:|:---:|
| **Footpaths** | | |
| Pathways are clearly defined | ✓ | ✗ |
| Surfaces to pathways are firm | ✓ | ✗ |
| Circle ✗ if loose gravel is provided as the surface finish | | ✗ |
| Circle ✗ if cobble stones or similar are provided as the surface finish | | ✗ |
| Surfaces are slip resistant in all weather conditions | ✓ | ✗ |
| The colour of the finish is uniform throughout | ✓ | ✗ |
| Circle ✗ if there are changes in colour which could appear as steps to people with poor vision | | ✗ |
| Open gaps in the surface finish (if any) are less than 10 mm wide | ✓ | ✗ |
| Maximum difference in level of surfaces (if any) does not exceed 5 mm | ✓ | ✗ |
| If the level of the path is higher than the adjacent ground: | | |
| there is a kerb of minimum height 100 mm provided which does not present a tripping hazard to users | ✓ | ✗ |
| OR | | |
| there is a tapping rail of minimum height 100 mm provided which does not present a tripping hazard to users | ✓ | ✗ |
| The kerb or tapping rail is visually contrasted with the path and the adjacent ground | ✓ | ✗ |
| **Width of footpaths** | | |
| The path is 1200 mm wide minimum | ✓ | ✗ |
| OR | | |
| The path is 1500 mm wide minimum | ✓ | ✗ |
| The path is 1800 mm wide minimum | ✓ | ✗ |
| **Gradient of footpath** | | |
| The gradient of the path is 1:20 or flatter | ✓ | ✗ |
| The cross fall gradient of the path is 1:50 or flatter | ✓ | ✗ |
| **Changes of direction** | | |
| Corners at changes of direction of the path are splayed or rounded | ✓ | ✗ |
| **Gratings** | | |
| Slots in gratings (if any) do not exceed 13 mm wide | ✓ | ✗ |
| Circular holes in gratings (if any) do not exceed 18 mm diameter | ✓ | ✗ |
| Drainage channels at dropped kerbs (if any) are protected with a flat plate across the channel for the full length of the dropped kerb | ✓ | ✗ |
| **Dropped kerbs** | | |
| The width of the dropped section of kerb is 1200 mm minimum | ✓ | ✗ |

| Item | Check | |
|---|:---:|:---:|
| OR | | |
| The width of the dropped section of kerb is 2000 mm minimum | ✓ | ✗ |
| The gradient at dropped kerbs is 1:15 or flatter | ✓ | ✗ |
| The appropriate use of tactile paving is made (in terms of colour, profile, size and design) | ✓ | ✗ |
| **Handrails (see also Stairs checklist)** | | |
| A suitable handrail (or balustrade) is provided at all changes of level | ✓ | ✗ |
| **Lighting** | | |
| The footpaths are provided with lighting | ✓ | ✗ |
| The lighting is provided which does not create areas of uneven lighting or strong shadows | ✓ | ✗ |
| The lighting provided enhances the visual definition of any potential hazards | ✓ | ✗ |
| **Street furniture** | | |
| Bollards (if provided) are a minimum 1000 mm high | ✓ | ✗ |
| Bollards (if provided) are adequately visually contrasted with the background against which they will be viewed: | | |
| for the full height | ✓ | ✗ |
| OR | | |
| for a minimum of 150 mm at the top of the bollard | ✓ | ✗ |
| Bollards used for car parking or to control entrances (if any) recess to be flush with the surface of the footpath or area when unlocked | ✓ | ✗ |
| All potential hazards (litter bins, planters, seats, signs, etc.) are logically placed | ✓ | ✗ |
| All potential hazards are visually contrasted with the background against which they will be viewed: | | |
| for the full height | ✓ | ✗ |
| OR | | |
| for a minimum of 150 mm at the top of the potential hazard | ✓ | ✗ |
| The minimum distance between pieces of street furniture is 1000 mm | ✓ | ✗ |
| For long or sloping journey routes, appropriate seating is provided every 100 metres | ✓ | ✗ |
| **Projections** | | |
| Plants, bushes and shrubs are managed such that they do not extend or project into the circulation route | ✓ | ✗ |
| There is a minimum 2100 mm clear headroom to any trees, bushes or other objects such as awnings, bay windows, etc. (if any) projecting into the line of the footpath | ✓ | ✗ |
| Projections below 2100 mm are protected with an upstand or tapping rail at least 100 mm high | ✓ | ✗ |
| There is clear evidence of appropriate management to the paths and the adjacent areas | ✓ | ✗ |

## Entrances and reception areas checklist

| Item | Check | |
|---|---|---|
| **The entrance** | | |
| The principal entrance to the building is accessible to everyone | ✓ | ✗ |
| The entrance is clearly distinguishable when approaching the building | ✓ | ✗ |
| A canopy providing adequate shelter is provided over the entrance doors | ✓ | ✗ |
| OR | | |
| The entrance doors are recessed | ✓ | ✗ |
| Transitional lighting is provided for people entering the building | ✓ | ✗ |
| **Entry systems (other than those controlling car parking)** | | |
| Entry systems are suitable for use by disabled people | ✓ | ✗ |
| The entry system incorporates an induction coupler | ✓ | ✗ |
| The entry system incorporates an LED or similar text display | ✓ | ✗ |
| Swipe card entry systems are appropriately positioned 750 mm to 1000 mm affl | ✓ | ✗ |
| The position of the entry system is logical | ✓ | ✗ |
| The position of the entry system is clearly identified using visual contrast | ✓ | ✗ |
| The top operational button of the entry is 1200 mm affl or less | ✓ | ✗ |
| Appropriately designed signage is provided with instructions on how to use the entry system | ✓ | ✗ |
| Appropriately designed signage is provided with instructions on how to get assistance if a disabled person cannot use the entry system | ✓ | ✗ |
| **Entrance doors** | | |
| The minimum clear opening width through one leaf is 800 mm | ✓ | ✗ |
| There is a 300 mm clear space beside the leading edge | ✓ | ✗ |
| The maximum pressure needed to open the doors is 30 N from 0° to 30° and 22.5 N from 30° to 60° of the opening cycle | ✓ | ✗ |
| Delayed action closers are provided | ✓ | ✗ |
| If the doors open outwards they are: | | |
| recessed | ✓ | ✗ |
| OR | | |
| the swing area is protected adequately to prevent collisions | ✓ | ✗ |
| Vision panels with a visibility zone extending between 500 mm and 1500 mm affl are provided | ✓ | ✗ |
| Where necessary, manifestation is provided at 1050 mm and 1500 mm affl | ✓ | ✗ |
| If provided, manifestation is effective at all times the building is in use | ✓ | ✗ |

| Item | Check | |
| --- | --- | --- |
| If glass doors are provided: | | |
| the frame contrasts with the surrounding wall/screen | ✓ | ✗ |
| OR | | |
| the presence of the doors is differentiated from the rest of the wall/screen | ✓ | ✗ |
| Edges of doors are clearly visible when held in the open position | ✓ | ✗ |
| Door furniture is distinguishable in terms of visual contrast with the door | ✓ | ✗ |
| Door handles can be reached, gripped and used with minimum effort | ✓ | ✗ |
| A kicking plate at least 400 mm deep is provided | ✓ | ✗ |
| **Automatic doors** | | |
| Automatic doors, either manually or automatically operated, are provided | ✓ | ✗ |
| Warning of the presence of the automatic doors is provided | ✓ | ✗ |
| Warning of the direction of opening of the automatic doors is provided | ✓ | ✗ |
| Opening and closing door speed is appropriate | ✓ | ✗ |
| Doors remain open for an appropriate time | ✓ | ✗ |
| Appropriate safety arrangements are provided to prevent doors closing if there is an obstruction | ✓ | ✗ |
| **Revolving doors** | | |
| Circle ✗ if revolving doors are provided | | ✗ |
| If a revolving door is provided, there is an alternative entrance with a clear opening width of 800 mm adjacent and clearly visible | ✓ | ✗ |
| Circle ✗ if the alternative door is not provided with an automatic opening device | | ✗ |
| Circle ✗ if the alternative door is not operational at all times when the revolving door is in use | | ✗ |
| **Thresholds** | | |
| The threshold is: | | |
| flush | ✓ | ✗ |
| OR | | |
| the maximum change of level for the threshold is 15 mm | ✓ | ✗ |
| **Doormats** | | |
| Circle ✗ if coir or other deep pile matting is provided | | ✗ |
| Mats are ribbed and capable of supporting the weight of a wheelchair | ✓ | ✗ |
| Mats are recessed | ✓ | ✗ |
| Circle ✗ if mats present a tripping hazard | | ✗ |
| Circle ✗ if mats are loose or not firmly fixed | | ✗ |
| Mats are of sufficient size to allow at least one revolution of the wheel of a wheelchair to pass over | ✓ | ✗ |

## Entrances and reception areas checklist (continued)

| Item | Check | |
|---|---|---|
| **Lobbies** | | |
| Lobbies, if any, are appropriately designed to allow easy access and egress for all users | ✓ | ✗ |
| **Exits** | | |
| All exits have the same level of accessibility as that described for Entrances above | ✓ | ✗ |
| **Reception areas: approach** | | |
| The approach to the reception area is smooth and level | ✓ | ✗ |
| Directional signage to identify the position of the reception area is appropriate in terms of provision and design | ✓ | ✗ |
| **Reception areas: seating** | | |
| A variety of seating in terms of seat height and with and without arms is provided | ✓ | ✗ |
| Seating is sufficiently robust to allow someone to use the arms as assistance when sitting or standing | ✓ | ✗ |
| Spaces are provided or can be created which allow wheelchair users to sit within the main seating area | ✓ | ✗ |
| Seating contrasts visually with all backgrounds against which it will be viewed | ✓ | ✗ |
| **Reception areas: lighting** | | |
| Lighting to the reception area is appropriate to allow easy communication and comfort for users | ✓ | ✗ |
| **Reception desks** | | |
| The reception desk is logically placed | ✓ | ✗ |
| The position of the reception desk is identifiable from the entrance to the building | ✓ | ✗ |
| There is sufficient manoeuvring space in front of the reception desk | ✓ | ✗ |
| A lowered section is provided to the reception desk | ✓ | ✗ |
| An adequate knee recess is provided to enable form filling at the seated position | ✓ | ✗ |
| Communication is possible across the desk from the standing or seated position | ✓ | ✗ |
| An induction loop is provided | ✓ | ✗ |
| If provided, the induction loop is operational at the time of the audit | ✓ | ✗ |
| If necessary, the completion of forms for all users is possible | ✓ | ✗ |
| Lighting at the desk is appropriate to allow the face of the receptionist to be clearly seen | ✓ | ✗ |
| AND | | |
| sufficient to enable the completion of any forms, etc. | ✓ | ✗ |
| Illuminance at the desk is controllable | ✓ | ✗ |
| Circle ✗ if a reflective glass screen is provided | | ✗ |
| There is evidence of staff training in disability awareness and clear lip speaking | ✓ | ✗ |
| Instructions are available in alternative formats | ✓ | ✗ |

## Horizontal circulation checklist

| Item | Check | |
|---|:---:|:---:|
| **Corridors and passageways** | | |
| Corridors have a minimum clear width of 1200 mm | ✓ | ✗ |
| If a building is frequently used by a significant number of wheelchair users the corridors are: | | |
| 1800 mm wide | ✓ | ✗ |
| OR | | |
| have appropriately placed passing places | ✓ | ✗ |
| In existing buildings where corridor widths are less than 1200 mm: | | |
| widening internal door openings is being considered | ✓ | ✗ |
| AND | | |
| consideration is being given to the provision of passing places | ✓ | ✗ |
| Circle ✗ if doors (other than to accessible toilets) open into the corridors | | ✗ |
| Corridors are splayed or rounded at corners | ✓ | ✗ |
| **Surfaces** | | |
| The floor surface finishes used are firm enough to be suitable for wheelchair users | ✓ | ✗ |
| Carpets (if provided) have a shallow, dense pile | ✓ | ✗ |
| The floor surface is matt or low reflectivity | ✓ | ✗ |
| Floor surfaces are slip resistant, especially when wet | ✓ | ✗ |
| Circle ✗ if the floor surface appears shiny and potentially 'slippery' | | ✗ |
| The pattern of any floor covering is plain or with a subtle pattern | ✓ | ✗ |
| Junctions between finishes are level and firmly fixed | ✓ | ✗ |
| Appropriate visual contrast is provided at the junction of the floor with the wall | ✓ | ✗ |
| Wall surfaces are smooth to the touch | ✓ | ✗ |
| Circle ✗ if the surfaces to the floor or walls adversely affect the acoustics | | ✗ |
| **Glazed walls, screens and doors** | | |
| Appropriately designed manifestation is provided to glass screens at 1050 mm and 1500 mm affl | ✓ | ✗ |
| **Handrails (see also Stairs and steps, internal and external checklist)** | | |
| A handrail is provided along the length of the corridors | ✓ | ✗ |
| **Internal doors** | | |
| The minimum clear opening width of all internal doors is 750 mm | ✓ | ✗ |
| If double doors are provided, the minimum clear opening width of one leaf of the doors is 750 mm | ✓ | ✗ |

## Horizontal circulation checklist (continued)

| Item | Check | |
|---|---|---|
| There is a minimum 300 mm clear space beside the leading edge | ✓ | ✗ |
| For doors on circulation routes: | | |
| the swing area is protected | ✓ | ✗ |
| OR | | |
| the doors are recessed | ✓ | ✗ |
| All door furniture (handles, kicking plates and finger plates) are distinguishable in terms of visual contrast from the door | ✓ | ✗ |
| Door handles are lever style with a return to the door on the open end | ✓ | ✗ |
| A 400 mm deep kicking plate is provided | ✓ | ✗ |
| The kicking plate is fixed with non-projecting fixings | ✓ | ✗ |
| The pressure required to open an internal door is less than 20 N | ✓ | ✗ |
| Delayed action door closers are provided | ✓ | ✗ |
| The delayed action door closers, if any, are operating correctly | ✓ | ✗ |
| Internal doors are clearly identifiable in terms of visual contrast with the surrounding wall | ✓ | ✗ |
| The leading edge of all internal doors is visually contrasted and is clearly visible when open | ✓ | ✗ |
| A vision panel is provided in internal doors which has a zone of visibility between 500 mm and 1500 mm affl | ✓ | ✗ |

**Fire doors**
Fire doors:

| | Check | |
|---|---|---|
| can be opened easily by disabled people | ✓ | ✗ |
| OR | | |
| are held open on electrically powered hold open devices linked to the fire alarm system | ✓ | ✗ |
| Checks have been undertaken to ensure fire doors held open on electrically powered open devices (or similar) can be opened by disabled people when activated to the closed position | ✓ | ✗ |

**Lobbies**

| | Check | |
|---|---|---|
| Internal lobbies, if provided, are appropriately designed to allow easy manoeuvrability | ✓ | ✗ |

**Lighting**

| | Check | |
|---|---|---|
| Illuminance in corridors is a minimum of 100 lux | ✓ | ✗ |

## Stairs and steps, internal and external checklist

| Item | Check | |
|---|:---:|:---:|
| **General information** | | |
| The stairs are made up of a straight flight or flights of stairs | ✓ | ✗ |
| Circle ✗ if the stairs are spiral or contain a section which has winders | | ✗ |
| Circle ✗ if the stairs have open risers | | ✗ |
| Circle ✗ if the stairs (including any landings) are not protected to the underside to prevent a user colliding with the stair | | ✗ |
| There are no more than 12 risers in each flight | ✓ | ✗ |
| The surface width of the stairs is a minimum 1200 mm | ✓ | ✗ |
| Corduroy pattern tactile flooring, which extends the width of the flight, is provided at the top and bottom of each flight | ✓ | ✗ |
| There is a change in floor texture at the top and bottom of each flight that gives adequate warning of the presence of the stairs | ✓ | ✗ |
| **Design, size and layout** | | |
| There is a clear landing of at least 1200 mm at the top of each flight | ✓ | ✗ |
| There is a clear landing of at least 1200 mm at the bottom of each flight | ✓ | ✗ |
| The risers on each step are the same dimension | ✓ | ✗ |
| The treads on each step are the same dimension | ✓ | ✗ |
| The height of the risers are between 150 mm and 170 mm | ✓ | ✗ |
| The going of the tread is between 250 mm and 300 mm | ✓ | ✗ |
| Circle ✗ if there are projecting nosings on the steps | | ✗ |
| **Handrails** | | |
| A handrail is provided to each side of the stair | ✓ | ✗ |
| On a wide flight of stairs a central handrail is provided | ✓ | ✗ |
| The handrail is between 40 mm and 50 mm diameter | ✓ | ✗ |
| OR | | |
| The handrail is oval with dimensions between 50 mm wide and 38 mm deep | ✓ | ✗ |
| The handrail can be gripped along its full length | ✓ | ✗ |
| There is a clear space of at least 60 mm between the handrail and the adjacent wall | ✓ | ✗ |
| The fixing to the handrail allows the hand gripping the rail to pass by the fixing without the fixing making contact with or injuring the user's hand | ✓ | ✗ |
| The handrail extends horizontally at least 300 mm beyond the first and last nosing in the flight | ✓ | ✗ |
| The handrail is continuous around landings | ✓ | ✗ |

## Stairs and steps, internal and external checklist (continued)

| Item | Check | |
|---|:---:|:---:|
| The top of the handrail is 900 mm to 1000 mm (measured vertically) above the nosings | ✓ | ✗ |
| The top of the handrail is 900 mm to 1100 mm (measured vertically) above landings | ✓ | ✗ |
| The material that the handrail is made of/covered with is timber or nylon or other material that is easy and comfortable to grip, smooth and not cold to the touch | ✓ | ✗ |
| Tactile information, indicating floor levels, etc., is used on the handrails | ✓ | ✗ |
| **Contrast** | | |
| The nosings on each step are adequately visually contrasted | ✓ | ✗ |
| The contrast extends 55 mm on the tread and the riser | ✓ | ✗ |
| The contrast to the nosings can be seen when ascending and descending the stairs | ✓ | ✗ |
| The handrails are adequately visually contrasted with the background against which they will be viewed | ✓ | ✗ |
| There is a tactile warning surface or a change of floor colour and texture at the head and foot of the stair that gives adequate warning of the presence of the stairs | ✓ | ✗ |
| **Lighting** | | |
| Illuminance at tread/floor level is a minimum of 200 lux | ✓ | ✗ |
| Circle ✗ if the lighting provided is in the risers of the steps | | ✗ |
| Circle ✗ if the lighting to the stairs is not even, causes glare, or is disorientating to users | | ✗ |
| **Maintenance** | | |
| The handrails are securely fixed to the supporting wall | ✓ | ✗ |
| Nosings are in good order | ✓ | ✗ |
| Circle ✗ if nosings present a tripping hazard or are in poor repair | | ✗ |
| The light fittings to the stairs are clean | ✓ | ✗ |
| **Additional for external steps only** | | |
| Circle ✗ if an 800 mm deep corduroy tactile surface is not provided at the top and bottom of each flight | | ✗ |

## Ramps, internal and external checklist

| Item | Check | |
|---|---|---|
| **Slope** | | |
| The travel distance on the slope is less than 10 metres | ✓ | ✗ |
| The slope rises vertically less than 500 mm over its length | ✓ | ✗ |
| If the slope is part of a series of ramps the total vertical rise is less than 2 metres | ✓ | ✗ |
| If the gradient does not exceed 1:20, the length of the ramp is less than 10 metres | ✓ | ✗ |
| If the gradient does not exceed 1:15, the length of the ramp is less than 5 metres | ✓ | ✗ |
| If the gradient is 1:12, the length of the ramp is less than 2 metres | ✓ | ✗ |
| Circle ✗ if any part of the ramp is steeper than 1:12 | | ✗ |
| **Width** | | |
| The minimum surface width of the ramp is 1500 mm | ✓ | ✗ |
| If the surface width of the ramp is less than 1800 mm, there is a clear unobstructed view along the whole length of the ramp | ✓ | ✗ |
| **Landings** | | |
| For a ramp that does not exceed 1:20, there is a level landing every 10 metres | ✓ | ✗ |
| For a ramp that does not exceed 1:15, there is a level landing every 5 metres | ✓ | ✗ |
| If an intermediate landing is provided, it is at least 1500 mm long | ✓ | ✗ |
| If a passing place is needed, a landing of at least 1800 mm by 1800 mm is provided | ✓ | ✗ |
| There is a level landing at least 1200 mm long at the top of the ramp | ✓ | ✗ |
| There is a level landing at least 1200 mm long provided at the bottom of the ramp | ✓ | ✗ |
| Circle ✗ if the landings at the top and bottom of the ramp could be encroached upon by the swing of a door | ✓ | ✗ |
| There is a level landing provided at each change of direction of the ramp | ✓ | ✗ |
| If uncovered, the cross fall to the landings is less than 1:50 | ✓ | ✗ |
| All landings will not allow water to stand on the surface | ✓ | ✗ |
| **Surfaces** | | |
| The surface to the ramp is: | | |
| smooth | ✓ | ✗ |
| AND | | |
| firm enough to take the load imposed on it | ✓ | ✗ |
| AND | | |
| slip resistant when wet | ✓ | ✗ |
| AND | | |
| easy to maintain | ✓ | ✗ |

## Ramps, internal and external checklist (continued)

| Item | Check | |
|---|:---:|:---:|
| If different surface finishes are used on the ramp, landings and approach paths, coefficients of friction of all surfaces are similar | ✓ | ✗ |
| Circle ✗ if a tactile warning has been provided at the top or bottom of the ramp | | ✗ |
| Circle ✗ if there is a surface pattern to the ramp (cross stripes, etc.) that could visually appear as steps | | ✗ |
| **Handrails** | | |
| A handrail is provided on the ramp | ✓ | ✗ |
| A handrail is provided on both sides of the ramp | ✓ | ✗ |
| If a very wide ramp is provided, there is a central handrail | ✓ | ✗ |
| The handrail is between 40 mm and 50 mm diameter | ✓ | ✗ |
| OR | | |
| The handrail is oval with dimensions between 50 mm wide and 38 mm deep | ✓ | ✗ |
| The handrail can be gripped along its full length | ✓ | ✗ |
| There is a clear space of at least 60 mm between the handrail and the adjacent wall (if any) | ✓ | ✗ |
| The fixing to the handrail allows the hand gripping the rail to pass by the fixing without the fixing making contact with or injuring the user's hand | ✓ | ✗ |
| The handrail extends horizontally at least 300 mm beyond the start and finish of the ramp | ✓ | ✗ |
| The handrail is continuous around landings | ✓ | ✗ |
| The top of the handrail is 900 mm to 1000 mm (measured vertically) above the surface of the ramp | ✓ | ✗ |
| The top of the handrail is 900 mm to 1100 mm (measured vertically) above surface of the landings (if any) | ✓ | ✗ |
| The material that the handrail is made of/covered with is timber or nylon or other material that is easy and comfortable to grip, smooth and not cold to the touch | ✓ | ✗ |
| **Alternative steps** | | |
| Circle ✗ if no steps are provided as an alternative to using the ramp | | ✗ |
| **Lighting** | | |
| Illuminance on the floor surface of the ramp is at least 200 lux | ✓ | ✗ |
| Light fittings are well maintained | ✓ | ✗ |
| Circle ✗ if the lighting to the ramp is not even, causes glare or is disorientating to users | | ✗ |

| Item | Check | |
|------|-------|--|
| **Temporary ramps** | | |
| Circle ✗ if it is possible to provide a permanent ramp | | ✗ |
| The surface of the temporary ramp is at least 800 mm wide | ✓ | ✗ |
| The surface is slip resistant and well drained | ✓ | ✗ |
| There is an upstand which prevents wheels slipping over the edge | ✓ | ✗ |
| The maximum gradient is 1:12 | ✓ | ✗ |
| The ramp is appropriately visually contrasted with the background against which it will be viewed | ✓ | ✗ |
| The ramp is well illuminated when in place | ✓ | ✗ |

For external steps see Stairs, internal and external checklist.


## Lifts checklist

| Item | Check | |
|------|-------|--|
| **Passenger lifts** | | |
| **Manoeuvring** | | |
| There is a manoeuvring space of at least 1500 mm by 1500 mm outside the entrance to the lift | ✓ | ✗ |
| The entrance door to the lift has a clear opening width of at least 800 mm | ✓ | ✗ |
| OR | | |
| In a building which may be used by sports wheelchairs, the entrance door has a clear opening width of at least 1000 mm | ✓ | ✗ |
| The minimum internal dimensions of the lift at floor level are 1100 mm by 1400 mm | ✓ | ✗ |
| Lift cars meet level with floors at all floors served by the lift | ✓ | ✗ |
| The floor surface inside the lift is firm and slip resistant | ✓ | ✗ |
| A handrail is provided on three sides inside the lift | ✓ | ✗ |
| If a handrail is provided, it can be gripped (40 mm to 50 mm diameter) | ✓ | ✗ |
| If a handrail is provided, it is located at 900 mm affl | ✓ | ✗ |
| **Calling the lift** | | |
| The position of the buttons to call the lift is logical | ✓ | ✗ |
| The call panel is clearly distinguishable in terms of visual contrast from its background | ✓ | ✗ |
| The buttons illuminate when pressed | ✓ | ✗ |
| The information on the buttons is appropriately embossed | ✓ | ✗ |
| The buttons are placed between 900 mm and 1200 mm affl | ✓ | ✗ |

## Lifts checklist (continued)

| Item | Check | |
|---|---|---|
| Lift arrival indication is given (using a text or a symbol) | ✓ | ✗ |
| An audible sound indicates the arrival of the lift | ✓ | ✗ |
| Circle ✗ if, in a bank of lifts, it is not clear which lift has arrived | | ✗ |
| **Using the lift** | | |
| The lift doors remain open for at least 5 seconds | ✓ | ✗ |
| The door reactivating device operates on infrared or photo eye sensors | ✓ | ✗ |
| Circle ✗ if the reactivating device operates on a pressure sensor | | ✗ |
| Audible warnings of the doors opening and closing are provided | ✓ | ✗ |
| The volume and clarity of the message is appropriate | ✓ | ✗ |
| Floor level indicators can be seen when the lift is full | ✓ | ✗ |
| Outside the lift, tactile and visual floor level indicators are provided which are clearly visible to users when the lift door opens | ✓ | ✗ |
| There is a mirror on the rear wall of the lift (above handrail level) | ✓ | ✗ |
| The mirror is of sufficient size to allow a wheelchair user to get information when reversing out of the lift | ✓ | ✗ |
| The mirror is of sufficient size to allow a wheelchair user to see a floor indicator placed above the door | ✓ | ✗ |
| The floor level arrived at is announced audibly and visually | ✓ | ✗ |
| **Controls within the lift** | | |
| The control panel is situated logically within the lift | ✓ | ✗ |
| The buttons are within easy reach by all users | ✓ | ✗ |
| Call or control buttons are located between 900 mm and 1100 mm affl | ✓ | ✗ |
| Call or control buttons are located at least 400 mm away from any return wall | ✓ | ✗ |
| Call buttons are 20 mm to 30 mm diameter (or equiv. if square or rectangular) | ✓ | ✗ |
| Information on the call buttons is provided in Braille | ✓ | ✗ |
| Information on the call buttons is embossed (1 mm) | ✓ | ✗ |
| Call buttons illuminate when pressed | ✓ | ✗ |
| Circle ✗ if the call buttons are touch sensitive | | ✗ |
| **Contrast and lighting** | | |
| The position of the lift is adequately identified using visual contrast and is well illuminated | ✓ | ✗ |
| Lighting within the car is a minimum 100 lux | ✓ | ✗ |

| Item | Check | |
|---|:---:|:---:|
| **Emergency equipment** | | |
| There is an alarm button fitted which is within easy reach for wheelchair users | ✓ | ✗ |
| Information of what to do in an emergency is provided | ✓ | ✗ |
| The information is provided in large print (sans serif font, min 12 point) | ✓ | ✗ |
| The information is also provided in Braille | ✓ | ✗ |
| There is an audible indication that assistance has been requested | ✓ | ✗ |
| There is a visual indication that assistance has been requested | ✓ | ✗ |
| If the emergency system relies on audible communication, it is supported by written text information explaining emergency procedures | ✓ | ✗ |
| OR | | |
| a text phone | ✓ | ✗ |
| If a telephone is provided, an induction coupler is fitted | ✓ | ✗ |
| **Generally** | | |
| The surface finishes used within the lift are not highly reflective | ✓ | ✗ |
| The surface finishes used within the lift do not create an unacceptable acoustic environment | ✓ | ✗ |

**Platform lifts**

| | | |
|---|:---:|:---:|
| If a platform lift is provided, compliance with the requirements of BS 6440:1999 has been checked | ✓ | ✗ |
| The platform lift has no enclosure and the rise is no greater than 2 metres | ✓ | ✗ |
| The platform lift has an enclosure and the rise is no greater than 4 metres | ✓ | ✗ |
| The minimum clear dimensions of the platform are 1050 mm wide by 1250 mm long | ✓ | ✗ |

**Wheelchair stair lifts**

| | | |
|---|:---:|:---:|
| If a wheelchair stair lift is provided, compliance with the requirements of BS 5776: 1996 Annex A has been checked | ✓ | ✗ |
| When parked, the stair lift leaves a clear unobstructed width on the stairs | ✓ | ✗ |
| When installed, the minimum clear width between the folded down platform and the handrail opposite is 600 mm | ✓ | ✗ |
| Circle ✗ if the installation of the platform lift results in the loss of one handrail on the stairs | | ✗ |
| A means of summoning assistance is provided | ✓ | ✗ |
| Any alarms provided comply with the requirements of ISO 9386-2 | ✓ | ✗ |

## WC facilities (standard and accessible) checklist

| Item | Check | |
|---|---|---|
| **Ambulant accessible toilet** | | |
| **Number of compartments** | | |
| There is at least one ambulant accessible compartment in each standard male toilet | ✓ | ✗ |
| There is at least one ambulant accessible compartment in each standard female toilet | ✓ | ✗ |
| **General spatial layout** | | |
| The internal dimensions of the compartment allow at least 750 mm activity space in front of the WC clear of door swings | ✓ | ✗ |
| **Doors** | | |
| The door to the cubicle opens outwards | ✓ | ✗ |
| If the door opens inwards, it can be opened outwards or removed easily in an emergency | ✓ | ✗ |
| **WC** | | |
| The WC is placed centrally across the width of the WC | ✓ | ✗ |
| The height of the seat is at 480 mm affl | ✓ | ✗ |
| The flush is a 'spatula' type | ✓ | ✗ |
| **Grab rails** | | |
| There are two horizontal (or 15° sloping) grab rails, each 600 mm long, placed 680 mm affl and with their centre line 650 mm from the rear wall of the cubicle | ✓ | ✗ |
| There is a 600 mm grab rail placed vertically on one side wall. The bottom of the rail is 800 mm affl | ✓ | ✗ |
| Grab rails protrude less than 90 mm into the cubicle space | ✓ | ✗ |
| If a urinal is provided for use by ambulant disabled people, a 500 mm grab rail is provided both sides of the urinal | ✓ | ✗ |
| **Lighting** | | |
| Lighting provides a minimum 100 lux | ✓ | ✗ |
| Circle ✗ if the lighting produces glare | | ✗ |
| **Other essential items** | | |
| A coat hook is provided at between 1200 mm and 1400 mm affl | ✓ | ✗ |
| There is evidence of appropriate, ongoing management for the day-to-day use of the facility (e.g. refilling, replacing essential items regularly) | ✓ | ✗ |

| Item | Check | |
|------|:---:|:---:|
| **Wheelchair accessible toilet** | | |
| **Accessibility** | | |
| Signage indicating the route to, and position of, the toilet facilities is adequate | ✓ | ✗ |
| Circle ✗ if a unisex accessible toilet that can be accessed independently of other toilet accommodation is NOT provided | | ✗ |
| Circle ✗ if entry into the accessible toilet is controlled by a RADAR key or some other method of locking | | ✗ |
| **General spatial layout** | | |
| Accessible WC clear floor area is 2200 mm by 1500 mm | ✓ | ✗ |
| The horizontal travel distance to an accessible toilet with an appropriate transfer side is less than 40 metres if on the same level | ✓ | ✗ |
| OR | | |
| 40 metres if the travel distance includes using a lift | ✓ | ✗ |
| In employment situations, an assessment has been made of the needs of the disabled employee/s to determine the suitability of the above dimensions | ✓ | ✗ |
| **Doors** | | |
| Door opens outwards | ✓ | ✗ |
| OR | | |
| Door opens inwards | ✓ | ✗ |
| Door can be removed easily in an emergency | ✓ | ✗ |
| **WC** | | |
| The centre line of the WC is 500 mm from the nearest wall | ✓ | ✗ |
| The space between the WC and the wall is kept clear to allow a carer to assist if required | ✓ | ✗ |
| The height to the top of the seat is 480 mm affl | ✓ | ✗ |
| The seat is suitable for heavy duty use (not a gap-front style) | ✓ | ✗ |
| The front of the WC projects 750 mm from the face of the supporting wall | ✓ | ✗ |
| The seat is securely fixed and of a good quality | ✓ | ✗ |
| There is a low-level cistern that could be used as a backrest | ✓ | ✗ |
| OR | | |
| A backrest with padded section has been provided 680 mm affl | ✓ | ✗ |
| The flush is a 'spatula' type | ✓ | ✗ |
| The flush is on the open transfer side | ✓ | ✗ |
| There is a single-sheet toilet paper dispenser within easy reach of the WC | ✓ | ✗ |
| There is a dispenser for hand wipes within easy reach of the WC | ✓ | ✗ |

## WC facilities (standard and accessible) checklist (continued)

| Item | Check | |
|---|---|---|
| **Grab rails** | | |
| There is a drop-down rail that is easy to operate from the seated position placed 350 mm from the centre line of the WC | ✓ | ✗ |
| There is a vertical grab rail that extends between 800 mm and 1400 mm affl and is placed to the open side of the WC, its centre line 470 mm from the centre of the WC | ✓ | ✗ |
| There is a grab rail on the wall adjacent to the WC that is 600 mm long and is placed 680 mm affl. One end of the grab rail is 250 mm away from the wall supporting the WC | ✓ | ✗ |
| There is a grab rail on the door at a height that will enable someone using a wheelchair to pull the door closed | ✓ | ✗ |
| There are two vertical grab rails, one either side of the wash hand basin, which extend between 800 mm and 1400 mm affl | ✓ | ✗ |
| The diameter of all grab rails is between 32 mm and 35 mm and they are easy to grip even when wet | ✓ | ✗ |
| **Washing and drying hands** | | |
| There is a wall-supported wash hand basin (not pedestal supported) basin provided with the top of the basin 720 mm to 740 mm affl | ✓ | ✗ |
| The basin can be reached and used easily whilst seated on the WC | ✓ | ✗ |
| The basin is 140 mm to 160 mm away from the WC | ✓ | ✗ |
| A single-lever mixer tap is provided | ✓ | ✗ |
| A soap dispenser is provided | ✓ | ✗ |
| The temperature of the water being delivered from the tap is controlled | ✓ | ✗ |
| The temperature of the water is appropriate | ✓ | ✗ |
| There is a paper towel dispenser that can be reached whilst seated on the WC | ✓ | ✗ |
| A manually operated (not proximity operated) warm-air dryer with the activation button max 1200 mm affl is provided adjacent to the hand basin | ✓ | ✗ |
| **Lighting** | | |
| A white pull cord for the light is provided adjacent to the door | ✓ | ✗ |
| OR | | |
| A device is installed which automatically switches on the light when the toilet door is opened | ✓ | ✗ |
| Lighting provides a minimum 100 lux | ✓ | ✗ |
| Circle ✗ if the lighting produces glare | | ✗ |

| Item | Check |
|---|---|
| **Alarm** | |
| An emergency alarm call system is provided | ✓ ✗ |
| A red alarm pull is fitted | ✓ ✗ |
| The alarm pull is provided with two red bangles which are either: | ✓ ✗ |
| 50 mm diameter | |
| OR | |
| open triangular with 50 mm sides | ✓ ✗ |
| One bangle is positioned 100 mm affl and one between 800 mm and 1000 mm affl | ✓ ✗ |
| The alarm is both audible and visual within the WC when activated | ✓ ✗ |
| There is a reset button provided which is clearly visible, signed and positioned such that it can be reached whilst seated in a wheelchair | ✓ ✗ |
| **Visual contrast** | |
| The sanitary fittings and facilities provide adequate visual contrast with their background | ✓ ✗ |
| The visual contrast at the junction of the floor with the walls is adequate | ✓ ✗ |
| **Other essential features** | |
| The floor covering is slip resistant (including when wet) | ✓ ✗ |
| A small shelf for use by colostomy users is provided | ✓ ✗ |
| Coat hooks are provided at 1050 mm and 1400 mm affl | ✓ ✗ |
| A mirror is provided above the hand basin | ✓ ✗ |
| A shaver point is provided adjacent to the mirror and between 800 mm and 1000 mm affl | ✓ ✗ |
| If provided in the standard toilet accommodation, vending machines are provided in the accessible toilet | ✓ ✗ |
| OR | |
| They are accessible in the standard toilets or reasonably in another place | ✓ ✗ |
| Wall tiles or finishes are non-reflective | ✓ ✗ |
| Facilities for disposable items are provided in a manner that does not impinge upon the manoeuvring space within the WC | ✓ ✗ |
| There is evidence of appropriate, ongoing management for the day-to-day use of the facility (e.g. refilling, replacing essential items regularly) | ✓ ✗ |

## WC facilities (standard and accessible) checklist (continued)

| Item | Check | |
|---|---|---|
| **Standard toilet facilities** | | |
| **Generally (in all cases)** | | |
| Signage indicating the route to, and position of, the toilet facilities is adequate | ✓ | ✗ |
| Visual contrast of all fittings with the background against which they will be viewed is appropriate | ✓ | ✗ |
| The visual contrast at the junction of the floor with the walls is adequate | ✓ | ✗ |
| Wall tiles or finishes are non-reflective | ✓ | ✗ |
| Lever mixer taps are provided | ✓ | ✗ |
| The temperature of the water being delivered from the tap is controlled | ✓ | ✗ |
| The temperature of the water is appropriate | ✓ | ✗ |
| The floor covering is slip resistant (including when wet) | ✓ | ✗ |
| Fitting such as flushes to WC and light switches are usable by people with restricted dexterity | ✓ | ✗ |
| Urinals are provided at a choice of heights affl | ✓ | ✗ |
| Facilities for washing and drying hands are reachable by all potential users | ✓ | ✗ |
| Lighting provides a minimum of 100 lux | ✓ | ✗ |
| There is evidence of appropriate, ongoing management for the day-to-day use of the facility (e.g. refilling, replacing essential items regularly) | ✓ | ✗ |

# Appendix B
# Information sources

## Guidance

**Access Audit Price Guide** BCIS, 2002

**Access for Disabled People** Sport England, 2001

**Accessible London: achieving an inclusive environment** GLA, 2004

**Accessible Thresholds in New Housing**: **guidance for house builders and designers** The Stationery Office, 1999

**Buildings for All to Use 2: improving accessibility of public buildings and environments** CIRIA, 2004

**Building Sight**: a handbook of building and interior design solutions to include the needs of visually impaired people RNIB, HMSO, 1995

**Code for Lighting** CIBSE, 2002

**A Design Guide for the Use of Colour and Contrast to Improve the Built Environment for Visually Impaired People** ICI Paints, 1997

**Designing for Accessibility** CAE, 2004

**Designing for Spectators with Disabilities** Sport England, 1992

**Disability: Making Buildings Accessible Special Report** Workplacelaw Network, 2005

**Diversity and Equality in Planning: a good practice guide** Heriot-Watt University & ODPM, 2005

**Easy Access to Historic Buildings** English Heritage, 2004

**Easy Access to Historic Landscapes** English Heritage, 2005

**European Concept for Accessibility** CCPT, 1996

**Guidance on the Use of Tactile Paving Surfaces** DTLR, 1999

**Inclusive Buildings** Blackwell Science, 2002

**Inclusive Mobility**: a guide to best practice on access to pedestrian and transport infrastructure DfT, 2002

**Inclusive Projects: a guide for best practice on preparing and delivering project briefs to secure access** DfT, 2003

**Overcoming the Barriers: providing physical access to historic buildings** CADW, 2002

**Planning and Access for Disabled People**: a good practice guide ODPM, 2003

**Sign Design Guide** Sign Design Society & JMU, 2000

## Legislation, standards and codes

Copies of the following legislation are available from The Stationery Office. The legislation can be viewed at www.legislation.gov.uk

**Disability Discrimination Act 1995 (DDA)** The Stationery Office, 1995

This is the principal statute. Note that this was varied by the Disability Rights Commission Act 1999, by Part 2 of the Special Educational Needs and Disability Act 2001 and by the Disability Discrimination Act 2005.

**Disability Discrimination Act 2005 (DDA 2005)** The Stationery Office, 2005

This amends the Disability Discrimination Act 1995.

**Disability Rights Commission Act 1999 (DRCA)** The Stationery Office, 1999

This set up the Disability Rights Commission (DRC). The major significance of the DRCA for our purpose is the responsibility that it places on the DRC to draw up and keep updated the Codes of Practice on behalf of the Secretary of State. The DRCA additionally amended certain parts of the DDA.

**Special Educational Needs and Disability Act 2001 (SENDA)** The Stationery Office, 2001

Part 2 of this Act extends the obligations not to discriminate to schools, higher and further education institutions and other providers of educational services. The act inserts new sections into the DDA and makes a variety of other minor changes.

**Statutory Instruments**

Statutory Instruments under the DDA can be viewed at www.legislation.gov.uk

The Codes of Practice relating to the DDA are available on the DRC website www.drc-gb.org

**Code of Practice, Rights of Access: Services and Premises** The Stationery Office, 2006

**Code of Practice, Supplement to Part 3 Code of Practice, Provision and Use of Transport Vehicles** The Stationery Office, 2006

**Code of Practice Employment and Occupation** The Stationery Office, 2004

**Code of Practice Trade Organisations and Qualifications Bodies** The Stationery Office, 2004

**The Duty to Promote Disability Equality Statutory Code of Practice, England and Wales** The Stationery Office, 2005

**The Duty to Promote Disability Equality Statutory Code of Practice, Scotland** The Stationery Office, 2005

**Code of Practice for Schools** The Stationery Office, 2002

**Code of Practice for Providers of Post-16 Education and Related Services** The Stationery Office, 2002

**The Building Regulations 2000 Approved Document M – Access to and Use of Buildings (England and Wales)** The Stationery Office, 2003

**The Building Regulations (Northern Ireland) 2000 Technical Booklet R: Access and facilities for disabled people** The Stationery Office, 2001

**BS 8300:2001 (incorporating amendment No. 1) Design of Buildings and their Approaches to Meet the Needs of Disabled People – Code of Practice** BSI, 2005

**BS 5588:Part 8:1988 Fire Precautions in the Design, Construction and Use of Buildings – Code of Practice for Means of Escape for Disabled People** BSI, 1988

**Human Rights Act 1998** The Stationery Office, 1998

**Equal Treatment Directive 1975** (amended 2002) The Stationery Office, 2002

## Useful organisations

**The Access Association**
Tel 01922 652010
www.accessassociation.co.uk

**Ann Sawyer Access Design** provides consultancy services, including access audits, access appraisals, access statements and training.
Tel 020 8444 2311
www.accessdesign.co.uk

**Building Cost Information Service Ltd (BCIS)**
Tel 020 7695 1500
www.bcis.co.uk

**Centre for Accessible Environments** provides information and advice, training and consultancy services.
Tel and textphone 020 7840 0125
www.cae.org.uk

**Center for Universal Design**: a research, information and technical assistance centre based at North Carolina State University.
www.design.ncsu.edu/cud

**Chartered Institution of Building Services Engineers (CIBSE)**
Tel 020 8675 5211
www.cibse.org

**Department for Transport Mobility and Inclusion Unit**
Tel 020 7944 6100
www.dft.gov.uk

**Disabled Persons Transport Advisory Committee (DPTAC)** advises the government on access for disabled people to transport. Their website has a useful access directory.
www.dptac.gov.uk

**Disability Rights Commission** is an independent body established by Act of Parliament to eliminate discrimination against disabled people. It provides information and advice, supports disabled people, campaigns to strengthen the law and provides an independent conciliation service for disabled people and service providers. The DRC also writes and produces the Codes of Practice relating to the DDA.
DRC helpline tel 0845 762 2633
www.drc-gb.org

**The Disability Unit at the Department for Work and Pensions**
www.disability.gov.uk

**Employers' Forum on Disability**
Tel 020 7403 3020
www.employers.forum.co.uk

**Is there an accessible loo? (ITAAL)** provides information on accessible WCs and publishes **The English Directory of Accessible Loos**.
www.itaal.org.uk

**National Register of Access Consultants**: a UK-wide accreditation service and register of access auditors and access consultants.
Tel 020 7735 7845
www.nrac.org.uk

**RADAR** provides general information on the needs of disabled people.
Tel 020 7250 3222; minicom 020 7250 4119
www.radar.org.uk

**Research Group for Inclusive Environments**
School of Construction Management and Engineering, The University of Reading, Whiteknights, PO Box 219, Reading RG6 6AW.
Tel 01189 316734; minicom 01189 864253
www.reading.ac.uk/ie

**Royal National Institute for the Blind (RNIB)** provides help, advice and support for people with visual impairments.
Tel 020 7388 1266
www.rnib.org.uk

**Royal National Institute for Deaf People (RNID)** provides help, advice and support for people with hearing impairments.
Tel 020 7296 8000; minicom 020 7296 8001
www.rnid.org.uk

**Sign Design Society**
Tel 01582 713556
www.signdesignsociety.co.uk

# Index

Page references in **bold** indicate figures or plates.

To save space in the index, the following abbreviations have been used:

BS, British Standard; DDA, Disability Discrimination Act